LESS STUDENT STRESS, MORE SCHOOL SUCCESS

Strategies and Activities for Creating Optimal Learning Environments Grades K–12

Susanna Palomares • Dianne Schilling

pro·ed
An International Publisher

8700 Shoal Creek Boulevard
Austin, Texas 78757-6897
800/897-3202 Fax 800/397-7633
www.proedinc.com

©2010 by PRO-ED, Inc.
8700 Shoal Creek Boulevard
Austin, Texas 78757-6897
800/897-3202 Fax 800/397-7633
www.proedinc.com

ISBN: 978-1-4164-0459-0

This book was developed by Innerchoice Publishing and Jalmar Press
in cooperation with the publisher, PRO-ED, Inc.

Printed in the United States of America

1 2 3 4 5 6 7 8 9 10   19 18 17 16 15 14 13 12 11 10

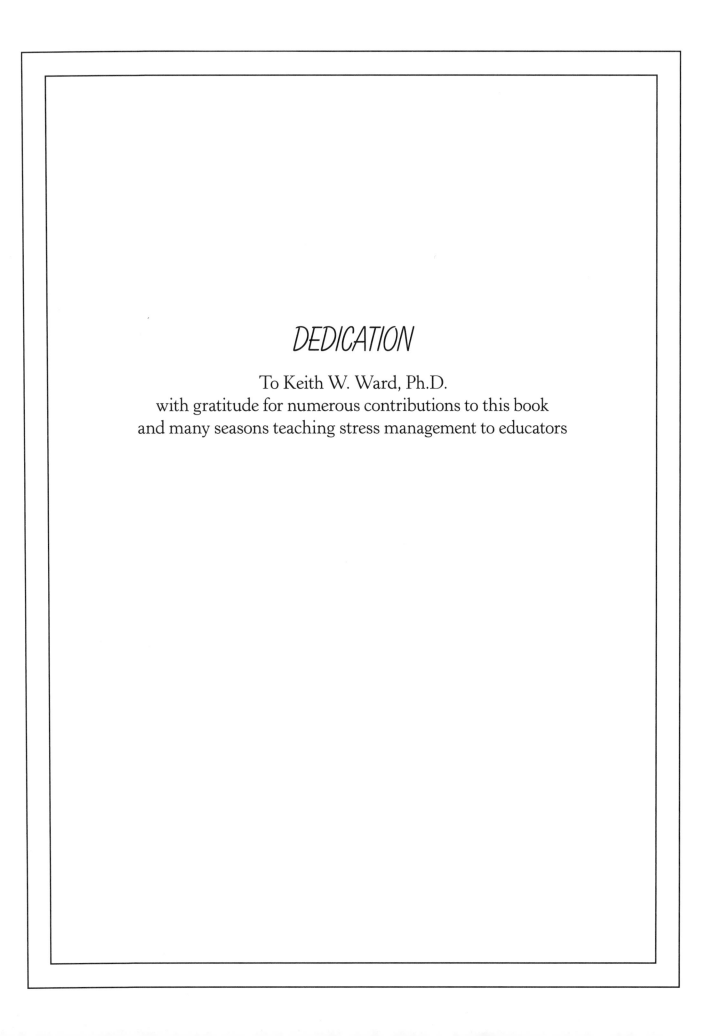

DEDICATION

To Keith W. Ward, Ph.D.
with gratitude for numerous contributions to this book
and many seasons teaching stress management to educators

CONTENTS

LESS STUDENT STRESS, MORE SCHOOL SUCCESS!
INTRODUCTION FOR TEACHERS AND COUNSELORS

Stress is part of every child's life. An argument with a friend, moving to a new neighborhood, a family breakup, tests, grades, pressure from parents—the parade starts early and never stops. However, contrary to popular belief, stress doesn't come from the outside. The report card, the test, and the divorce are the stressors. The stress itself is in the child's response to those incidents. Stressors are the daily events that challenge a child to adapt. Stress is the child's response as he or she attempts to make the adjustment, which is why the manifestations of stress are so variable from person to person, child to child.

Children benefit from some stress. Writing a report, preparing for an exam, rehearsing for a performance—all demand the stimulation of positive stress, which can help a child perform at his or her best. But stress can also be damaging. It can turn into distress. It can eat away at a child and consume so much energy that performance declines. Stress in the right proportions is a life enhancer. Excessive, prolonged stress is a life destroyer.

You will never eliminate stress from your classroom or counseling practice, nor should you. Stress management doesn't mean getting rid of all stress. It means helping kids understand the stress response, identify individual and collective stressors, and learn and practice effective strategies for reducing stress and minimizing its destructive consequences. That in a nutshell is the purpose of this book.

UNDERSTANDING THE STRESS RESPONSE

Humans have inherited a physiological stress-response better suited to fending off attacking lions than coping with the stresses of modern life. During emergencies, a flood of hormones accelerates heart rate and breathing and rushes oxygen and nutrients to active muscles so that we can either defend ourselves against the perceived danger or beat a hasty retreat. At the same time, other bodily functions, including digestion, pain perception, and the immune system slow down or stop. The types of emergencies for which our ancestors evolved this "fight or flight" response were usually over quickly. Either they made it to safety or became somebody's dinner. In contrast, the stresses we face today, though rarely life threatening, tend to be recurring and persistent. School pressures, family squabbles, money worries, minor disagreements, tests, grading, and hundreds of other features of everyday life can produce the pounding headache, queasy stomach, racing heart, and sweaty palms we associate with stress. Furthermore, the stress response may kick in over and over again throughout a typical day.

The main stress hormones involved in the stress response are *epinephrine* (better known as *adrenaline*) and the steroid hormone *cortisol*. Epinephrine acts in seconds, while cortisol backs up epinephrine over minutes or hours. It's the longer acting cortisol that most often leads to health problems, as it tends to linger in the system long after the stressful event is over (which may explain why a person still agitated from one stressful encounter tends to react more easily to the next one). The brain activates the stress response whether a child actually experiences something stressful or just thinks about it.

EFFECTS ON HEALTH AND LEARNING

Stress compromises the immune system and increases vulnerability to viral infections such as the common cold. The scientific link between stress and colds is compelling—and just the tip of the iceberg. Stress triggers asthma attacks, raises blood pressure, exacerbates heart disease, contributes to ulcers and colitis, and worsens chronic pain. Furthermore, stress can short circuit memory, impede learning, and permanently damage the brain.

In **Brain Rules** (2008, p. 178), molecular biologist John Medina observes:

> *Stressed people don't do math very well. They don't process language very efficiently. They have poorer memories, both short and long forms. Stressed individuals do not generalize or adapt old pieces of information to new scenarios as well as non-stressed individuals. They can't concentrate. In almost every way it can be tested, chronic stress hurts our ability to learn.*

Memory and information are stored in neural networks—vast arrays of connected neurons. Learning and storing memories involves the strengthening of some branches rather than others in the network. Much of the action takes place in the cortex and the hippocampus of the brain, both vital to memory. In **Why Zebras Don't Get Ulcers** (1998), neuroscientist Robert Sapolsky uses this simple computer analogy to illustrate the relationship between the two: The cortex is like our hard drive, where memories are stored, and our hippocampus is the keyboard, the means by which we place and access memories in the cortex.

Sapolsky explains that short-term stress, if not too severe, can enhance memory by spurring glucose delivery to the brain and making more energy available to neurons. You may remember every detail of the circumstances surrounding your first kiss, or receiving news of the Challenger explosion, or the World Trade Center disaster. These are examples of short-term stress enhancing memory formation and retrieval.

There are dozens, probably hundreds of neurotransmitters that pass information across the synapses between neurons. The most important one in the cortex and hippocampus is *glutamate*. Glutamate works a little differently than other neurotransmitters. Instead of a small amount of glutamate causing a little bit of neural excitation (and, thus, a little bit of learning), a small amount often produces no effect at all (no learning). A little more glutamate, and still no response. A nonlinear threshold of excitation must be reached before learning is achieved. As that connection continues to be reinforced at the threshold level, eventually it is "potentiated," which means that the synapse has learned something.

Memory is disrupted when stress becomes too great or prolonged. Not only do learning and memories fail to occur, they may actually be depressed, so that we start forgetting things as well. Glucose delivery to the hippocampal areas of the brain subsides, too, so the brain gets less energy. Memory and concentration are seriously compromised during times of stress.

So just as a child is struggling to perform well on the SAT, the long-term potentiation and nourishment of hippocampal neurons are being reduced. With even more sustained stress, cortisol actually begins to damage neurons. With prolonged stress, axons and dendrites in neural networks begin to shrivel, atrophy, and retract. As the complexity of neural networks declines, so does a child's ability to access stored information. The memories may still be there, but it takes longer to retrieve them.

There is also growing evidence that severe stress may lead to the permanent loss of hippo-campal neurons (Sapolsky, 2004). MRIs of people with post-traumatic stress disorder (PTSD), including victims of physical and sexual abuse and people with severe depression, have shown major and selective atrophy of the hippocampus. In many cases the tests were completed long after the trauma occurred, suggesting that the damage may be permanent.

Accelerated learning experts have recognized for decades that stress inhibits learning and have consistently promoted the use of relaxation exercises like visualization and music to reduce stress and increase energy levels prior to and during learning sessions (Jensen, 2000). More recently, the "mindfulness" movement has successfully advocated the routine use of breathing exercises, progressive relaxation, and a variety of classroom interventions to help manage student stress (Lantieri, 2008). These techniques help all students—especially the anxious ones—cope with stress more effectively.

SYMPTOMS AND COPING STRATEGIES

Most of us associate stress with the responsibilities of adulthood—going to work, paying the bills, keeping relationships on an even keel. We don't often realize that children are subjected to many of the same stressors that gnaw at us, and perhaps a good many more that we know nothing about. Childhood is anything but carefree for kids whose families are dysfunctional or disintegrating, who are exposed to domestic violence, surrounded by gangs and drugs, spend hours alone while their parents work, or are poorly nourished, and emotionally neglected. And, as we know from our own lives traumatic events are by no means the only sources of stress. Social pressures, school performance, peer teasing and bullying, and over-scheduling by super-competitive parents can leave a child exhausted.

Some children experience extremely high levels of performance anxiety. Every test is a crucible of their competence as a person. Excessive anxiety can interfere with attention and also with memory. When the stress reaches an intolerable threshold, some kids become phobic about school, skipping classes, or inventing illnesses and injuries in order to stay home.

In *Building Emotional Intelligence* (2008), author Linda Lantieri points out that symptoms of unmanaged stress in children are often mislabeled as inappropriate behavior requiring disciplinary action. Teachers and parents reprimand children for actions that are really stress reactions, rather than intentional misbehavior. Signs of stress may include:

- Increased physical illness (headaches, stomachaches, chronic fatigue)
- Withdrawal from people and activities
- Anger and irritability
- Sadness, tearfulness
- Worry
- Nervousness
- Difficulty sleeping
- Difficulty concentrating

The 2008 national KidsPoll conducted by the Nemours Foundation in collaboration with Southern Illinois University and numerous health agencies and reported at KidsHealth.org asked children ages 9 to 13 what things caused them the most stress. Top categories were: grades, school, and homework (36 percent); family (32 percent); and friends, peers, gossip, and teasing (21 percent).

The same poll found that children rely on a variety of coping strategies to handle stress. For example, 52 percent of kids reported playing or doing something active when stressed. Other popular strategies were listening to music (44 percent), watching TV or playing video games (42 percent), talking with a friend (30 percent), trying not to think about the problem (29 percent), trying to work things out (28 percent), and talking to a parent (22 percent). Potentially negative strategies included eating (26 percent), cutting, banging, or otherwise hurting themselves (25 percent), losing their temper (23 percent) and crying (11 percent).

AN ECLECTIC APPROACH TO STRESS MANAGEMENT

Activities that promote social-emotional learning (SEL) form an optimal foundation for school stress-reduction programs. Children who develop awareness of feelings, thoughts, and behaviors, who master their emotions, build effective communication and relationship skills, and learn to manage conflict are in a much stronger position to effectively cope with the perils of everyday stress. In the 1970s and 1980s, it was the affective education and self-esteem movements that led the way in teaching social-emotional skills. More recently, SEL has become a principal focus of the push to develop emotional intelligence and mindfulness in children. In his foreword to Linda Lantieri's (2008) book, *Building Emotional Intelligence*, Daniel Goleman equates SEL with "the systematic classroom teaching of emotional intelligence." He argues that helping children master their emotions and relationships makes them better learners.

Less Student Stress, More School Success approaches stress management broadly. Activities help students to understand the effects of stress on the brain, take steps to de-stress the learning environment, identify sources of stress, practice breathing and relaxation exercises, adopt habits that promote successful learning, understand the effects of nutrition and exercise on stress, and learn to more effectively manage anger and worry.

Getting kids involved. Having a sense (or illusion) of control over one's circumstances has been shown to alleviate stress. This is a tough one for kids, because they don't often have the power or resources to take matters into their own hands. However, even very young students can participate in establishing classroom rules and procedures, building both a sense of control and the commitment necessary to ensure success. We've included several activities that involve students in creating a more stress-free learning environment by identifying ways to achieve a state of "relaxed alertness" throughout the school day.

You can further increase student involvement and sense of control by listening "actively" when students exhibit distress, by helping children label their emotions and build a feeling vocabulary, and by teaching them how to use problem-solving to resolve stressful issues and conflicts. Older students can be taught to change their reactions to stressful events, promoting a lower heart rate, deeper breathing, clearer thinking, and feelings of calmness and control. The child who fakes a sprained ankle in order to avoid a stressful school environment is exerting some degree of control over her situation, but needs to learn better ways of coping.

Recognizing stress. When stress is pervasive, it's tempting to conclude that chronic tension and anxiety are normal states while serenity is rare. Instead of a smooth road with an occasional bump, life becomes a rough road with an occasional rest stop. Before kids become habituated to stress, we need to help them distinguish between ordinary conditions and stressful ones, so that they know stress when they see and feel it. Therefore, several activities in this book are devoted to helping students recognize the physical, emotional, and behavioral signs of stress, identify individual sources of stress, and link emotional highs and lows to stressful events.

Learning to cope. The largest group of activities in the book is dedicated to helping students identify, evaluate, and practice various approaches to managing stress, including common coping strategies like those identified by the KidsPoll and several relaxation exercises. The students conduct interviews with adults and peers; experiment with humor, laughter, and foveal vision; relax to music; and practice mindfulness through deep breathing, meditation, and progressive muscle relaxation.

The goal of mindfulness activities is to relax the body while focusing the mind. Systematic lessons and regular practice result in numerous benefits, including these five described by Lantieri (2008):

1. Increased self-awareness and self-understanding
2. Greater ability to relax the body and release physical tension
3. Improved concentration and ability to pay attention, which is critical to learning
4. Ability to deal with stressful situations more effectively
5. Greater control over thoughts, with less domination by unwelcome thoughts

A dose of prevention. One of the best ways to manage distress is to keep it from happening in the first place. By learning and practicing proven success strategies—life skills such as goal-setting and time management—students perform better in school and function more effectively in relationships. Acquiring life skills builds greater confidence, and greater confidence increases resilience in the face of all kinds of stressful events and circumstances. Several success strategies are addressed by activities in this book. Children learn to monitor their self-talk, use positive affirmations to reduce anxiety, set short and long-term goals, use time-management tools, and identify sources of help and support in the school, neighborhood, and community. In addition, several activities help students cope more effectively with the stress produced by high-stakes testing.

Managing anger. Anger is a common symptom of stress. Anger is also a stressful emotion, regardless of what triggers it. It is destructive to the health of the child who experiences it and, when expressed negatively or violently, to those on the receiving end as well. Furthermore, anger is a kind of default emotion, erupting swiftly when a child's feelings are intense and confused but he or she lacks the ability to accurately label them. As children gain emotional intelligence, incidents of anger subside, in part because kids learn to recognize and deal with the frustration, fear, embarrassment, jealousy, humiliation, and other feelings that so often precede anger. *Less Student Stress, More School Success* includes activities designed to help students understand the potential health consequences of anger, identify symptoms and triggers of anger, complete self-monitoring logs, role play anger-inducing scenarios, and commit to anger-management strategies.

Health and fitness. Exercise is one of the most popular and effective ways of relieving stress and, like healthful eating, serves a protective function as well. Being physically fit builds endurance and helps kids weather stressful conditions and maintain normal body weight. Activities in this book help kids set fitness goals, make positive lifestyle choices, explore various forms of exercise, calculate their working heart-rate range, and increase flexibility through stretching. In addition, students study food pyramids and nutrition-facts labels, develop meal and snack menus, and examine personal eating habits.

REFERENCES

Jensen, E. (2000). *Learning smarter: The new science of teaching.* San Diego: The Brain Store.

Lantieri, L. (2008). *Building emotional intelligence: Techniques to cultivate inner strength in children.* Boulder, CO: Sounds True.

Medina, J. (2008). *Brain rules: 12 principles for surviving and thriving at work, home, and school.* Seattle: Pear Press.

Sapolsky, R. (2004). *Why zebras don't get ulcers: An updated guide to stress, stress-related diseases, and coping.* New York: W.H. Freeman

What kids say about: Handling stress. (2008). Retrieved Dec. 18, 2008, from http://kidshealth.org

USING THE ACTIVITIES

Less Student Stress, More School Success is designed to be used at all grade levels, so an occasional modification may be necessary to optimize the activities for your students. The level of difficulty among the activities also varies slightly. If you like an activity, but think that the presentation is too sophisticated for your students, look for ways to modify it. Simplify the vocabulary, revise the explanations, and give examples that the children will find familiar. Adjust the activities to suit the maturity, reading ability, cultural background, and interests of your students.

Many of the activities are accompanied by reproducible "experience sheets" for the students to complete in class or, in a few cases, as homework. Several activities have two experience sheets, one for younger students and one for older students. Choose whichever form works best for you.

We've grouped the activities by topic area and arranged them in an order that makes sense to us, however most of the activities will stand alone and may be implemented in any order you choose. We recommend that you integrate the activities within your regular lesson plans, adding them wherever they seem appropriate. Once you've introduced the relaxation and breathing exercises, try to repeat them often, or substitute similar exercises from other sources. Make relaxation a regular part of the classroom and school routine.

Every activity includes a list of open-ended, thought-provoking discussion questions. These questions are a vital component of the activity. During discussion, students translate experiential learning into cognitive understanding and commit concepts to long-term memory. If you omit the discussion following an activity, you run the risk of weakening the experience. If the questions seem irrelevant based on what your students experienced while completing the activity, come up with new ones that build on the lessons they learned.

YOUR INCREDIBLE BRAIN

LIONS, TIGERS AND TESTS, OH MY!
RESEARCHING THE STRESS RESPONSE

OBJECTIVES   Students will:
- Understand the "fight or flight" response.
- Distinguish between short- and long-term stressors.
- Explain how stress affects health and learning.

MATERIALS   For research: computers with Internet access and/or library resources dealing with stress

DIRECTIONS   Ask for a show of hands from students who have done the following today:
- Wrestled a bear.
- Forged a raging river.
- Fought a rival for a hunk of meat.
- Swerved their bike to avoid being hit by a car.
- Had a fistfight with another kid.

Explain that these are examples of short-term stressors—emergencies that require fast action, but are over relatively quickly. Ask the students to think of other short-term stressors. Write their suggestions on the board.

In your own words, explain why the body's stress response, which is built to handle intense, short-term stress, has a tough time dealing effectively with the kinds of subtle, long-term stressors most people face today. Suggested script:

You are equipped with a "fight or flight" response that reacts to real or perceived emergencies by pouring a powerful mix of hormones into your bloodstream to speed up pulse and breathing, fuel muscles, and prepare you to defeat or escape the enemy. The problem is, if the enemy is not a tiger but a test, those same hormones, instead of helping you pass the test, can easily produce a headache, a stomachache, an inability to concentrate, or temporary memory loss. If severe and prolonged, stress can change the wiring of your brain—permanently.

Like it or not, all of us have inherited a physiological stress-response that's a little out of whack with today's world. If we were members of a primitive tribe living on the African plains, it would be perfect. Imagine hoisting your spear as a lion charges out of the bush. Your brain releases a flood hormones that prepare you to either run away or stand your ground and fight (which is why it's called the "fight or flight" response). You get a huge burst of energy. Your muscles tense. Your heart rate and breathing speed up, rushing more oxygen and nutrients to your muscles so that you can run faster or fight harder. At the same time, other bodily functions, such as digestion, slow down or stop.

This type of emergency is usually over quickly. Either you make it to safety or you become somebody's dinner. The problem is, it's not lions and tigers we have to worry about. Tests, chores, money problems, annoying siblings, and bullies are more like it. In today's world, the "fight or flight" response kicks in not just during times of physical danger, but over and over again throughout a typical day. School pressures, family squabbles, money worries, minor disagreements, tests, grading, public speaking, dating, and hundreds of other features of everyday life can produce the pounding headache, queasy stomach, racing heart, and sweaty palms associated with stress.

Explain to the students that the hormones and chemicals released in response to stress can build up in the system if the stress continues for more than a short time; for example, if they worry all year about grades. In your own words, explain:

Your nervous system releases a stress hormone called epinephrine that acts in seconds. Glucocorticoids (also known as cortisol) are steroid hormones that back up epinephrine over hours or days. It's these longer acting hormones that most often lead to health problems because they tend to linger in your system long after the stressful event is over. This may explain why, when you are still upset from one stressful event, you tend to react more easily to the next one.

The brain activates the stress response whether you actually experience something stressful or just think about it. For example, just thinking about an upcoming test can be as stressful as taking it. This continuous bombardment can damage your health. Stress compromises your immune system and increases your vulnerability to colds and other viral infections. Stress can trigger asthma attacks, raise blood pressure, aggravate heart disease, contribute to ulcers, and worsen chronic pain. It can also short circuit memory and impede learning.

Have the students form teams of two or three and research different aspects of the stress response. For example, have some teams learn more about epinephrine and cortisol. Have others research the link between stress and illness, and still others look at the effects of stress on learning. Arrange to have the teams report their findings to the class over the coming days or weeks.

DISCUSSION QUESTIONS

1. What are some examples of long-term stress that you, or someone you know, have experienced?
2. Have you ever been frightened by a sudden noise or something scary and felt the effects of stress hormones racing through your bloodstream? What did it feel like?
3. Why is vigorous exercise a particularly good way to relieve stress?
4. Why is the brain sometimes called the "master gland" of the body?
5. What is the most interesting thing you learned from your research?
6. How will what you learned affect the way you handle stress in the future?

STRESS AND THE BRAIN
DEMONSTRATION, SKITS AND DISCUSSION

OBJECTIVES Students will:
- Understand how neural networks are formed in the brain.
- Demonstrate how memory is stored and retrieved.
- Dramatize the effects of stress on learning and remembering.

MATERIALS The answers to three or four test questions written on slips of paper (choose age-appropriate, challenging questions in any academic subject area); one copy of the experience sheet "Brain Basics" for lower-grade students; one copy of the experience sheet "How Stress Batters the Brain" for upper-grade students

DIRECTIONS Distribute the experience sheets. Read through the information with the class. Facilitate discussion by describing examples of stressful situations that affect learning and memory (tests, public speaking, being called on in class, etc.) Conduct the following demonstration at any appropriate point during the discussion.

Demonstration

Ask four volunteers to come to the front of the room. Direct them to stand arm's length apart in a single line, facing the class. Have them stretch out their arms at shoulder level so that their fingers almost touch. Go down the line and quickly adjust positions to allow about six inches of space between the outstretched fingers of neighboring students. Tell the students to drop their arms to their sides.

Ask the class to imagine that each of these four students is a neuron in the brain. Their left arms are dendrites and their right arms are axons. Have the "neurons" stretch out their arms and wiggle their fingers. Walk down the line as you demonstrate how information from one neuron travels to the edge of its axon (fingertips), where it is released into the synapse (space between fingers) to be picked up by the dendrite (fingertips) of the next neuron.

Announce that the volunteers are going to demonstrate how the brain supplies an answer to a test question from memory.

Ask the first question of the entire class. Place the answer in the left (dendrite) hand of the end student. Have that student silently look at the answer, then switch it to his or her right hand (axon) and pass it to the left (dendrite) hand of the next student. Have that student and the third student repeat the process until the answer reaches the fourth student. Ask that person to read the answer aloud to the class.

Explain that the actual process is much more complicated, involving perhaps thousands of neurons in different parts of the brain. But no matter how many neurons are involved, the steps are basically the same. Information travels through the brain to a central point where it forms a memory—and an answer to the question.

Now choose a fifth volunteer to play the role of "STRESS." Ask another question, start the answer moving from one neuron to the next, but this time have "Stress" use one hand to block the passage of the answer across the first, second, and/or third synapse. Make several attempts to deliver the answer. Then coach "Stress" to become a "really big stressor" and use his or her whole body to block the passage of the answer, forcing the dendrites and axons to pull back, or completely withdraw. Explain that this is what happens when stress is severe and prolonged. If the stress is bad enough, neurons may be permanently damaged and drop completely out of the neural network. The result is loss of memory.

Have the students form teams of five and develop skits demonstrating the effects of different kinds of stress on neural networks. Encourage them to clarify where the "Stress" is coming from by giving the "Stress" a script to act out. Urge the teams to be creative in finding additional ways to dramatize that process. Have the teams perform their completed skits for the class.

DISCUSSION QUESTIONS

1. Have you ever tried to read a book while feeling worried about something? What was it like?
2. What is the "stress response" and what causes it?
3. Why do things like tests, music recitals, oral reports, speeches, and dance performances produce a stress response?
4. What can you do to lower your stress levels at times like these?
5. How does studying and being prepared help reduce school stress?

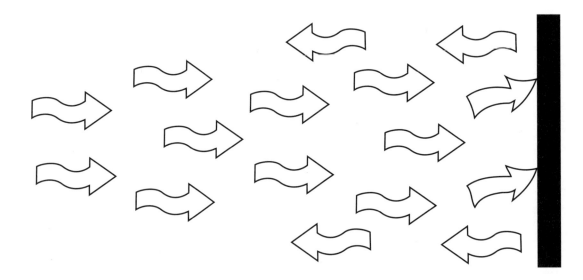

Less Student Stress, More School Success

HOW THE BRAIN LEARNS

- Your brain has about 100 billion nerve cells, called *neurons*.
- Each neuron has branches called *dendrites* and *axons*. These connect one cell to another.
- Neurons communicate by sending chemical and electrical messages to each other.
- Messages go across the gap between an axon of one cell to a dendrite of another. This gap is called a *synapse*.
- Messages travel like this from neuron to neuron.
- When you learn, you create new connections between brain cells. These connections help you get smarter.

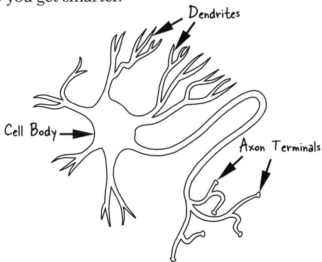

HOW STRESS AFFECTS LEARNING

- A little bit of stress is okay. It gives you energy and makes you more alert.
- Too much stress makes it hard to concentrate. It's tough to learn when you feel stressed.
- Stress can make you forget things—like the answers to test questions that you knew before the test.
- Stress causes the axons and dendrites that carry information between neurons to shrink and pull apart. When the stress is gone, the connections usually grow back.
- Staying stressed for too long can make you more vulnerable to colds and other illnesses. It can also cause permanent damage to memory.

HOW STRESS BATTERS THE BRAIN
EXPERIENCE SHEET

HOW THE BRAIN LEARNS

- Your brain has about 100 billion active nerve cells, called *neurons*.
- Neurons consist of a cell body, *dendrites* and *axons*. Each of your neurons connects with thousands of other neurons.
- Neurons process information by exchanging chemical and electrical messages.
- An electrical charge travels from the cell body down to the tip of the axon. Neurotransmitters (chemical messengers) are released from the tip of the axon into the synapse, the gap between two neurons. This triggers electrical energy in the receptors of the neighboring dendrite, which pick up the message.
- This process is repeated as the message travels from neuron to neuron, stimulating dendritic growth, or *branching*.
- The key to getting smarter is to grow more synaptic connections between brain cells. You do this by studying, practicing, and learning new information. These connections allow you to solve problems and perform well in school, sports, and other pursuits.

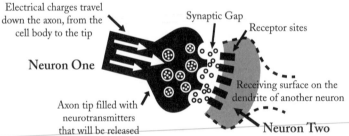

Electrical charges travel down the axon, from the cell body to the tip

Synaptic Gap

Receptor sites

Neuron One

Receiving surface on the dendrite of another neuron

Axon tip filled with neurotransmitters that will be released

Neuron Two

HOW STRESS AFFECTS LEARNING

- A little bit of stress can be helpful. It makes you more alert and provides extra energy.
- Too much stress can make you feel disorganized and unable to concentrate. It's tough to learn new information when you are stressed.
- Stress interferes with memory. It can cause you to forget someone's name, or the answer to a test question that you thought you knew. The frustration of not remembering produces even more stress.
- Stress causes the axons and dendrites that carry information across the synapses between neurons to shrivel and pull apart. The number of connections in your neural network declines and, with it, your memory.
- Staying stressed for too long can make you more vulnerable to colds and other illnesses.
- Post Traumatic Stress Disorder (PTSD), which is caused by very severe stress, can actually kill brain cells. In wartime, many soldiers end up with PTSD.

 Less Student Stress, More School Success

A MATTER OF TASTE
A THOUGHT EXPERIMENT

OBJECTIVES Students will:
- Experience the power of imagination to produce physical sensations.
- Describe how various thoughts produce emotional reactions.
- Recognize how thoughts alone can cause stress.

MATERIALS None

DIRECTIONS Tell the students that you are going to have them test the power of their imaginations. Ask them to sit relaxed at their desks with their hands on the desks and feet flat on the floor. Next, ask them to close their eyes and listen carefully as you slowly read the following directions:

Imagine a bright yellow lemon sitting in front of you on your desk. Imagine that you are picking up the lemon. Feel it's rough skin. The lemon is full of juice and you can feel its weight. Now imagine that you have a sharp knife in one hand. With the other hand, hold the lemon steady as you safely cut the lemon in half. Notice the sour juice that drips out of the lemon and onto your desk. Smell the pungent odor of the juice. Pick up half of the lemon. Feel the juice dripping into the palm of your hand and running down your wrist. Lift the lemon to your nose and smell it. Now, take a big bite out of the lemon. (Pause) Open your eyes.

Ask the students to describe any feelings and sensations they experienced as they imagined holding, cutting, and eating the lemon. Typical responses are, "I had a sour taste in my mouth," "My jaw felt funny," and "My mouth watered."

Ask the students who volunteer to explain how such reactions are possible, since there was never any lemon in the first place. Use their responses to spark a discussion about the power of imagination. Make these points:

- If your mouth watered at the thought of eating the lemon, your stomach probably secreted enzymes to neutralize the acid in the lemon juice. Your body may have reacted in other ways that you were unaware of, too.

- Your brain reacted to your thoughts about the lemon just as if the lemon were real. In the past, when you tasted a real lemon, your brain stored the memory of its flavor and your reaction. When you have experienced something and reacted in a certain way, just the thought of it can make you react in the same way again.

• Stress memories operate in the same way. Just the thought of a stressful event can cause your body to react as if that event were actually happening. Your brain doesn't discriminate between real and imagined stressful events. It sends out the same flood of hormones in either case.

DISCUSSION QUESTIONS

1. If you had never tasted a lemon, what do you think you would experience?
2. How do you react when someone tells a scary story?
3. What is something that you feel anxious just thinking about?
4. What is something that you feel embarrassed just thinking about?
5. What can you do to reduce the stress caused by imagined fears?

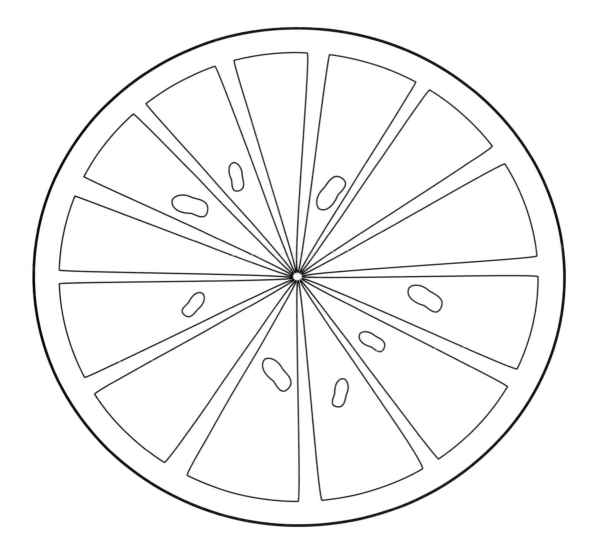

Less Student Stress, More School Success

THE POWER OF THOUGHT

USING THOUGHTS TO CHANGE FEELINGS AND BEHAVIOR

OBJECTIVES Students will:
- Recognize how thoughts affect feelings.
- Change negative thoughts to positive thoughts.
- Demonstrate how negative self-talk produces negative behavior, and positive self-talk produces positive behavior.

MATERIALS None

DIRECTIONS List the following words on the board:

Situation   Thought   Feeling   Behavior

Using the headings as a visual guide, explain to the students that in many situations, what they *think* and *say* about the situation heavily impacts how they *feel* about the situation and what they *do* (their behavior) as a result of the situation.

To illustrate this point, have the students close their eyes and listen carefully while you read the following situations, demonstrating the impact of contrasting reactions to the same event.

Rained Out

Response A

Situation: A trip to your favorite theme park is canceled because of heavy rain.
Thought: "That really sucks. The whole day is ruined. There's nothing to do (etc.)."
Feeling: Angry, disappointed, miserable, bored
Behavior: Mope around. Talk sullenly to everyone. Accomplish little or nothing.

Response B

Situation: A trip to your favorite theme park is canceled because of heavy rain.
Thought: "We will go in good weather. Today's a great day to read (etc.)."
Feeling: Optimistic, confident, creative, content
Behavior: Enjoy indoor activities. Talk pleasantly to others. Get a lot done.

A Pop Quiz

Response A

Situation: Your teacher surprises the class by giving an unannounced math quiz.
Thought: "I don't know this stuff. This isn't fair. I'm going to fail."
Feeling: Angry, pessimistic, low energy
Behavior: Complain. Get a slow start. Do poorly on the quiz.

Response B

Situation: Your teacher surprises the class by giving an unannounced math quiz.
Thought: "This will show me what I need to work on. I'll do the best I can."
Feeling: Accepting, determined, optimistic
Behavior: Pay attention. Focus on the questions. Pass the test.

Have the students open their eyes. Ask them: "How did thoughts affect feelings and actions in these examples?" Facilitate discussion, in the process making these points:

• Thoughts are easier to control than feelings.
• Since thoughts often produce feelings, many times we can change our feelings by changing our thoughts.
• When thoughts and feelings change, behavior usually changes, too.
• We are responsible for what we think, how we feel, and what we do.

Have the students form teams of four. Give each team one of the following situations (or other situations that you create). Explain that each team will create two short plays dramatizing their situation. The first play will demonstrate the effects of negative thoughts. The second will demonstrate the effects of positive thoughts. Urge the teams to refer to the headings on the board. Their job is to show how negative thoughts, and then positive thoughts, produce contrasting feelings and behaviors.

Situations

• Giving a speech to the class
• Attending a teacher conference with your parent
• Playing in a championship game
• Learning a new sport
• Not being invited to a party
• Doing homework

Have each group perform its contrasting plays, back-to-back, for the class. Facilitate discussion after each performance.

DISCUSSION QUESTIONS

1. How did thoughts influence feelings in this play? How did they influence behavior?
2. Have you ever changed your feelings about something by changing your thoughts? Tell us what happened.
3. What is one negative thought that you often have that you could change?
4. How difficult is it to change your thoughts about something?
5. Who is responsible for your thoughts? What about your happiness?

BRICKS AND BALLOONS
EXERCISING THE IMAGINATION

OBJECTIVES   Students will:
- Experience the power of imagination to influence behaviors.
- Describe how thoughts produce feelings and behaviors.
- Understand the connection between imagination (thoughts) and stress levels.

MATERIALS   None

DIRECTIONS   Ask the students to stand and space themselves evenly around the room. Give them the following directions, while you demonstrate the process, checking to see that everyone's hands are correctly positioned:

Stretch your hands out in front of you at shoulder height. Turn the palm of your left hand so that it is facing up toward the ceiling. Turn the palm of your right hand so that it is facing toward the floor. Close your eyes. Keep your eyes closed and hold this position until I tell you to open your eyes.

Take a deep breath and relax. Imagine that your left hand is holding a very heavy, dark red brick. Feel its weight. Now, imagine a large, helium-filled balloon floating above you and tied to your right wrist with a string. Look up and see the brightly colored balloon. Feel it pulling against your wrist as it tries to rise to the ceiling. Feel the brick pressing down on your left hand, forcing it toward the floor. Notice the weight of the brick getting heavier and heavier in your left hand. Feel the string tugging lightly on your right wrist as the balloon attempts to rise higher. The balloon wants to rise. The brick wants to fall. The balloon is light. The brick is heavy. The balloon is pulling on your right hand, while the brick is pressing heavily on your left hand.

Tell the students to open their eyes and look around the room. Ask them what they notice. Most of the students will have moved their hands involuntarily during the experiment, lowering their left hand (the one with the brick) and lifting their right hand (the one with the balloon). Give the students a few moments to comment on what they observe. Then have them take their seats and discuss the results.

Emphasize the power of imagination to influence behavior, even in the absence of conscious awareness. The brain-body is just as likely to react to imagined conditions as it is to real conditions. The high incidence of imagined fears and anxieties makes this particularly relevant to stress management. Help students understand that by changing their thoughts, they can often change their feelings and bodily reactions, which in turn can reduce stress.

DISCUSSION QUESTIONS

1. About how many inches did your hands move during the experiment?
2. What do you think caused your hands to move?
3. Were you aware that you were moving your arms and hands?
4. How did your left hand and arm—holding the brick—feel?
5. How did your right wrist and arm—holding the balloon—feel?
6. What did you learn about your imagination from this experiment?

Adapted from an activity by Keith Ward, Ph.D.

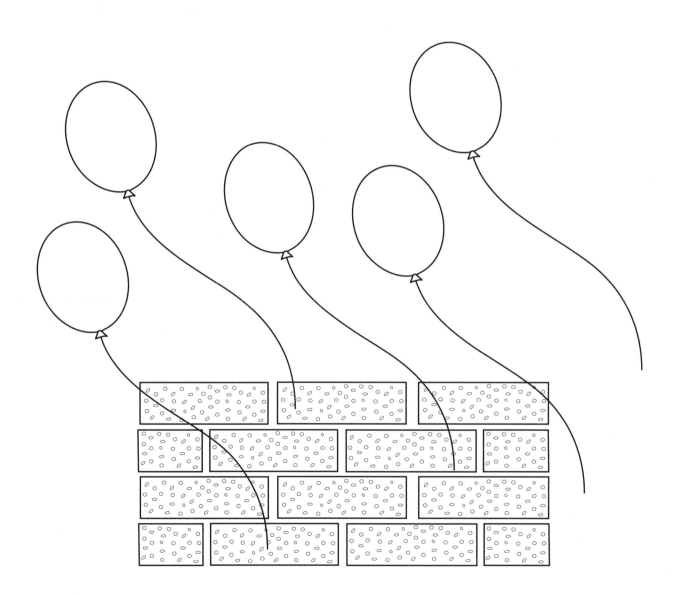

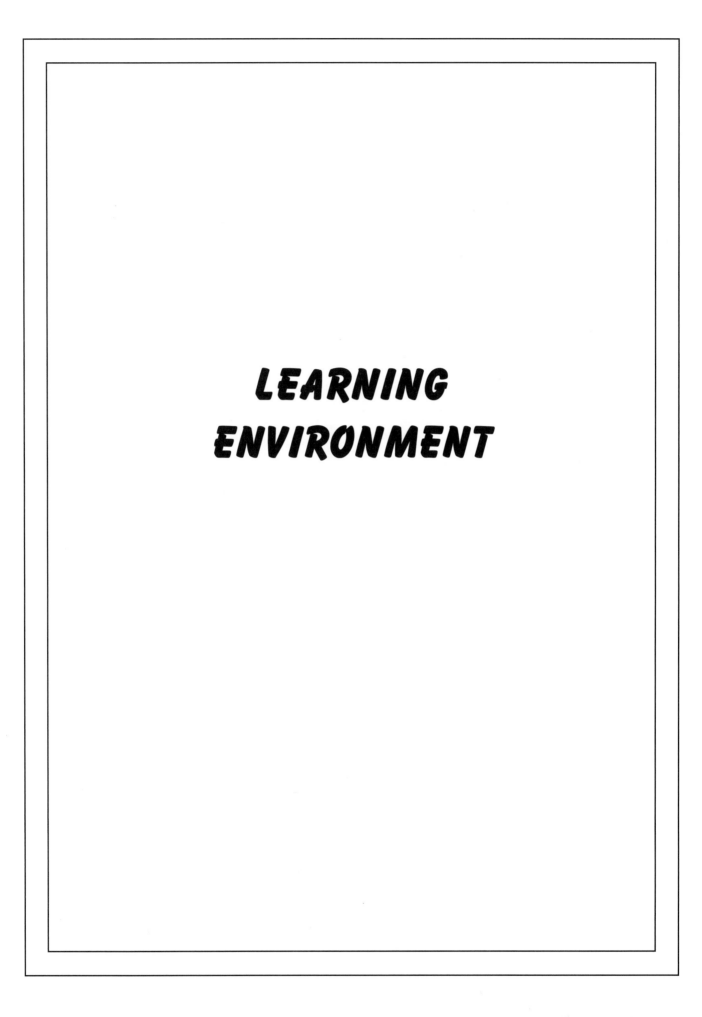

LEARNING ENVIRONMENT

RELAXED AND ALERT

HOW RELAXED ALERTNESS (R-A) AFFECTS PERFORMANCE

OBJECTIVES   Students will:
- Describe and compare feelings of relaxation and alertness.
- Identify situations in which they felt both relaxed and alert.
- Discuss benefits associated with relaxed alertness.

MATERIALS   Chart paper or white board, and markers

DIRECTIONS   Ask for a show of hands from students who feel relaxed "at this very moment."
Call on two or three and ask, "How do you know that you are relaxed?" Encourage
the students to describe the feelings and physical sensations that indicate relaxation,
such as feeling calm, loose-limbed, peaceful, pleasant, and well.

Next, ask for a show of hands from students who are alert "at this very moment." Repeat
the process, asking volunteers, "How do you know that you are alert?" Elicit feelings
such as focused, aware, wide awake, and attentive. Throughout the discussion, help the
students broaden their feeling-word vocabulary by suggesting and defining appropriate
new words.

Explain to the students that people learn best and remember what they learn longer
when they feel both relaxed and alert while they are learning. (Remind the class of
any students who shared that they felt relaxed and also shared that they felt alert during
the initial sharing.) State:

*Feeling relaxed can open your mind. It can boost your curiosity and make you eager and
interested. Feeling alert can help you pay attention and stay focused so that your senses
—your eyes and ears — take in more information. Experiencing both at the same time
sets the stage for optimal learning.*

Continue the discussion until most of the students grasp the concept of relaxed alertness
at a level appropriate to their age and experience. Then ask the students
to close their eyes and recall a time when they felt both relaxed and alert. State:

*Think of a time when you were totally relaxed and at ease and, at the same time,
completely concentrated on the task at hand. You might have been completing a puzzle,
drawing a picture, solving math problems, or shooting baskets. The task may have been
difficult or easy, but because you were both relaxed and alert, it probably felt enjoyable
and you made good progress. When you think of something, recall as much as you can
about the incident and your feelings.*

Ask several volunteers to share their experiences of relaxed alertness. As each volunteer briefly describes an incident, write key words on the board (or chart paper) under the heading "Situation." Then ask the volunteers how they know that they were both relaxed and alert in the situations. Record their comments in a second column under the heading "How I Know I Was Relaxed and Alert." Ask discussion questions (below) to help the students describe characteristics of the incidents, including outcomes, benefits and, especially, their feelings. Conclude the activity with a general discussion summarizing what the group learned about relaxed alertness.

DISCUSSION QUESTIONS

1. What feelings or sensations did you have in your body during the incident you described?
2. What emotions did you experience?
3. How much time passed during the incident? Did it seem like a long time, or a short time?
4. What did you learn from the incident?
5. How much of what you learned do you remember today?
6. How did you feel about your performance in the situation? Was it a good job?
7. What does it take to feel both relaxed and alert in a situation? How can you make it happen more often?
8. What can we do to increase relaxation and alertness in our classroom?

Adapted from an activity by Keith Ward, Ph.D.

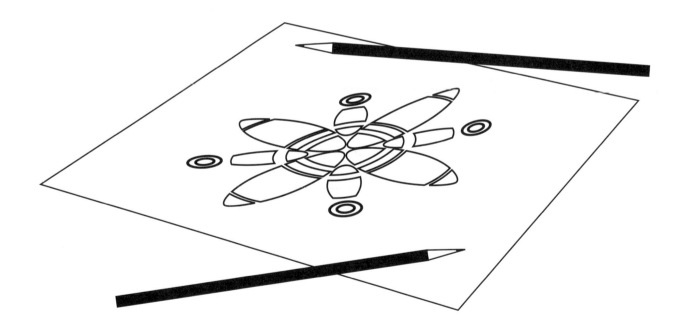

Less Student Stress, More School Success

R-A IN THE CLASSROOM

DEVELOPING A PLAN FOR RELAXED ALERTNESS

OBJECTIVES

Students will:
- Share ideas for increasing relaxed alertness in the classroom.
- Develop a plan for implementing relaxed-alertness strategies.

MATERIALS

One copy of the experience sheet "Bright Ideas for Relaxed Alertness" for each student; one copy of the summary sheet for each team of four; chart paper or white board, markers

DIRECTIONS

Remind the students of the previous activity highlighting the benefits of relaxed alertness. Tell them that you would like their help in developing a plan to increase relaxed alertness in the classroom so that everyone will not only feel better, but learn more easily and effectively. State:

All of us can contribute in some way. For example, everyone might feel more relaxed if study and reading periods were quieter, or if soft music were playing in the background. Alertness might increase if we all got at least eight hours of sleep every night, or if we worked in teams more often. There are many ways to increase relaxation and alertness. See how many ideas you can think of.

Distribute the experience sheets and go over the directions. Give the students a few minutes to individually complete the sheet.

Have the students form teams of three or four. Tell each group to select a recorder. Distribute summary sheets to the recorders. Instruct the groups to take turns sharing the ideas they wrote on their experience sheets. Have the recorders write all ideas on the summary sheet, eliminating duplications.

Encourage the teams to discuss the ideas on their lists, adding details and refinements.

When the teams have finished sharing (15 to 30 minutes), have the recorders take turns reading their lists to the entire group while you record ideas on the board or chart paper.

Go back over the final list and discuss individual items with the group. Eliminate items that are impossible to implement and circle items that are feasible and promising. See if you can get buy-in from the students on at least five items to try. If any of the five items requires an action plan, appoint a committee to work on it and set aside the necessary planning time. <u>Note</u>: Be sure to capture the final list on paper.

DISCUSSION QUESTIONS

1. Which idea on the final list will be the most difficult to achieve? Why?
2. Which will be the easiest to achieve? Why?
3. How can we help each other stick to the plan and make it work?
4. How do you feel about coming to this classroom every day? How would you like to feel?
5. Who wins when we make our classroom a great place to learn?

Adapted from an activity by Keith Ward, Ph.D.

Less Student Stress, More School Success

BRIGHT IDEAS FOR RELAXED ALERTNESS
EXPERIENCE SHEET

You learn best when your mind and body feel *relaxed* — not tense, worried, or uptight. It also helps to be *alert* — wide awake, listening, and interested. Feeling both relaxed and alert at the same time is especially cool.

What can we *all* do to make the classroom a better place to learn? What things will help us feel relaxed and alert? Write three ideas here:

1. _____

2. _____

3. _____

Shhhh...
Relaxed, Alert Students
at Work

What can *you* do to make the classroom a better place to learn? Do you need to change a behavior? Could you do more of something, or less of something? List three ideas here:

1. _____

2. _____

3. _____

BRIGHT IDEAS FOR RELAXED ALERTNESS
SUMMARY SHEET

List your team's ideas for increasing relaxed alertness and making the classroom a better place to learn.

1. _____
2. _____
3. _____
4. _____
5. _____
6. _____
7. _____
8. _____
9. _____

List your team's ideas for things that individual students can do. Add a check mark to an idea each time it is suggested by a different student.

1. _____
2. _____
3. _____
4. _____
5. _____
6. _____
7. _____
8. _____
9. _____

 Less Student Stress, More School Success

R-A ON DISPLAY

CREATING A POSTER DISPLAY OF THE PLAN

OBJECTIVES Students will:
- Create posters illustrating specific strategies for achieving relaxed alertness.
- Group the posters in a semi-permanent display.
- Demonstrate their commitment to the plan.

MATERIALS The final list of ideas for increasing relaxed alertness in the classroom (from the previous activity); large sheets of poster board; construction paper in various colors, scissors, marking pens, glue, and miscellaneous decorative materials; computers and publishing software (if available)

DIRECTIONS Display the final list of ideas for improving the learning environment through relaxed alertness (from the previous activity). If more than a few days have elapsed since the list was generated, spend a few minutes reviewing the concept and benefits of relaxed alertness.

Announce that the students will be working in small teams to create posters illustrating the agreed-upon strategies from the final list. When the posters are finished, another team will assemble them in a single display showing the entire plan. The semi-permanent display will remind and motivate everyone to stick to the plan. <u>Note</u>: If any of the teams will be creating computer-generated posters, arrange the logistics.

Have the students form teams of no more than three members each. Assign each team one of the ideas from the final list of strategies. Duplications are okay. Suggest that the teams take a few minutes to brainstorm words, pictures, symbols, and other graphics that convey their strategy. For example, "Sleep 8 Hours Every Night," could be illustrated with the face of a clock, a sleeping head on a pillow, a spiral of ZZZZZ's of different sizes and colors, and a poem or quotation about sleep. Some of the items could be drawn directly on the poster board, and others cut from colored construction paper, or illustrated on bold construction-paper shapes.

Distribute the art materials, or have the students select what they need from a central location. Teams that are using computers will want to review available clip art and photographs.

When the teams are ready, have them take turns sharing their finished products with the entire group. (This might need to occur in a follow-up session.)

Take a few minutes to brainstorm ideas for the final display. Encourage the students to think creatively. In addition to a bulletin-board display, think of ways to create a free-standing three dimensional display, or to group posters in mobile-like arrangements that can be hung from the ceiling. Choose three or four enthusiastic students to make the final decision and build the display.

DISCUSSION QUESTIONS

1. Why is it helpful to be relaxed while you are learning?
2. How does being alert help you to learn?
3. How many of you were relaxed and alert while making your posters?
4. Can you be relaxed and angry at the same time? What about relaxed and scared?
5. How does being tired affect alertness? What about being hungry?
6. How can we help each other be more relaxed and alert, more of the time?

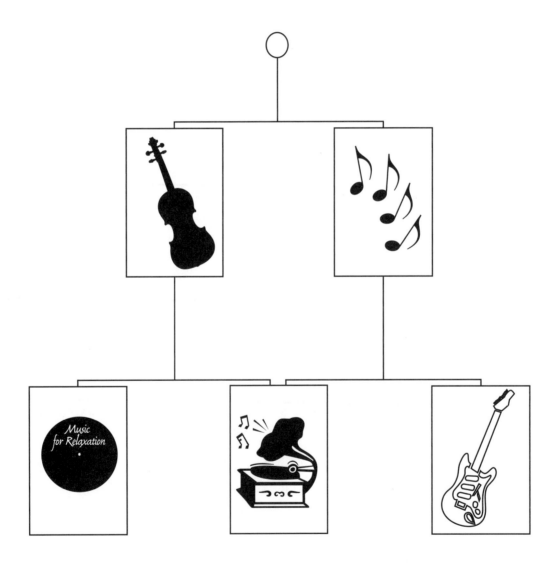

THUMBS UP, THUMBS DOWN
EVALUATING THE PLAN

OBJECTIVES   Students will:
- Rate the success of the relaxed alertness plan.
- Evaluate their own behavior on each of the plan's strategies.

MATERIALS   The relaxed alertness display, or list of strategies, from previous activities

DIRECTIONS   Talk briefly about the importance of evaluation to planning. State:

Anytime we make a plan, it's important to check regularly to ensure that all steps in the plan are being done correctly and on time. For example, when your family plans a special event or vacation, somebody has to check to make sure each person is doing his or her part to get ready. If we don't evaluate progress, the plan may fail. We have a plan to create a better learning environment in our classroom. But it may not work if we don't check once in awhile to make sure that we are doing what the plan says.

Explain that approximately once a week, the students will take a few minutes to assess their progress on the plan for increasing relaxed alertness. You will make statements about different parts of the plan, and they will indicate whether they agree or disagree with those statements. However, rather than call out their opinions, or vote, they will show their opinions with hand signals.

Demonstrate and explain the following signals:

Signal	Meaning
1. Thumb up and tracing circles in the air	Strongly agree
2. Thumb up and stationary	Agree
3. Thumb down and stationary	Disagree
4. Thumb down and tracing circles	Strongly disagree

Conduct the first evaluation by making one or two statements about each part of the plan. If possible, always refer to the display as you are doing this (see previous activity) to reinforce the display as a symbol of the plan and to give the evaluation process a visual anchor.

Vary your statements based on behaviors that you have observed during the previous week. Some statements should refer to overall class behavior and some to individual behavior. Here are a few sample statements:

- We practice good listening and don't interrupt.
- We are quiet during reading periods.

- We treat everyone in class with respect.
- I get at least eight hours of sleep every night.
- I remember to take several deep breaths to relax before quizzes.

Conclude the activity by reinforcing adherence to parts of the plan that are going well, and discussing how to improve on parts that are not going well. In some cases, the plan may need to be modified slightly, or changed.

DISCUSSION QUESTIONS

1. How can we do better on the parts of the plan that need improvement?
2. What parts of the plan are easiest to follow? Why?
3. What parts of the plan are hardest to follow? Why?
4. Do we need to change or delete any parts of the plan? Which ones?
5. What do you personally need to do better in order to help the plan succeed?

Adapted from an activity by Keith Ward, Ph.D.

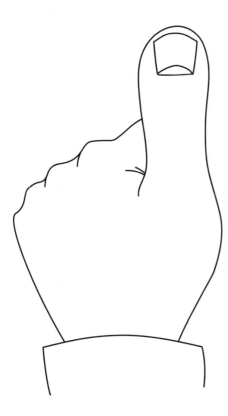
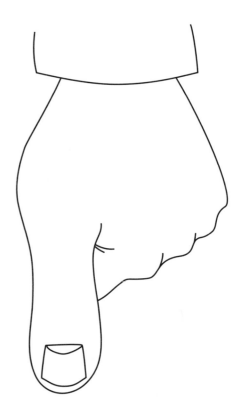

IDENTIFYING STRESSORS

THE EFFECTS OF STRESS

PHYSICAL, PSYCHOLOGICAL, AND BEHAVIORAL RESPONSES

OBJECTIVES   Students will:
- Distinguish between physical, psychological, and behavioral responses to stress.
- Describe specific responses in each area.

MATERIALS   None

DIRECTIONS   Write the following three headings on the board or chart paper: *Body, Mind, Behavior.* Explain to the students that stress affects people in all three areas. It causes physical responses, most of which are uncomfortable. It triggers thoughts and feelings, most of which are unpleasant. And it prompts us to take action — sometimes positive action, but often negative action.

Ask the students to help you brainstorm a list of physical responses to stress. Encourage them to recall how their bodies feel when something stressful happens. Write suggestions under the heading "Body." Add the following if they are not mentioned by the group.

- Racing heart
- Shaking, shivering
- Sweating, or feeling cold
- Upset stomach
- Headache
- Tense muscles
- Loss of appetite, or urge to overeat
- Inability to sleep
- Dry mouth and throat
- Difficulty speaking

Under the "Mind" heading, brainstorm a list of thoughts, feelings, and other psychological reactions to stress. Include:

- Feeling down, gloomy
- Feeling out of control
- Getting upset easily
- Self-criticism
- Forgetfulness
- Inability to concentrate
- Fearfulness, anxiety

Under the "Behavior" heading, brainstorm a list of actions that are often provoked by stress. This list could include both negative and positive behaviors, since both are common. Distinguish between the two by underlining or circling positive behaviors. Include:

- Angry outbursts
- Arguing
- Crying (can be either negative or positive)
- Hurting others
- Isolating (avoiding friends, family)
- Talking it over
- Exercising
- Sleeping
- Staying busy (homework, chores, hobbies)

Point out that everyone reacts to stress differently. Some of us are more sensitive to stressful situations than others. We react more quickly and more intensely. Others of us are more volatile. We get defensive and angry very easily. Still others seem able to ignore stressful conditions except in the extreme. Furthermore, just because we feel irritable or have a headache doesn't mean we are under stress. But if we experience several of these reactions at the same time, we ought to consider what might be causing us stress.

Conclude the activity with additional discussion.

DISCUSSION QUESTIONS

1. Which of these reactions do you most often experience?
2. What do you say to yourself when you react in negative ways?
3. What is the worst stressful reaction you can remember having?
4. What did you do about it and how long did it last?
5. What is the best response to stress you can remember having?
6. How quickly did it help, and in what ways?

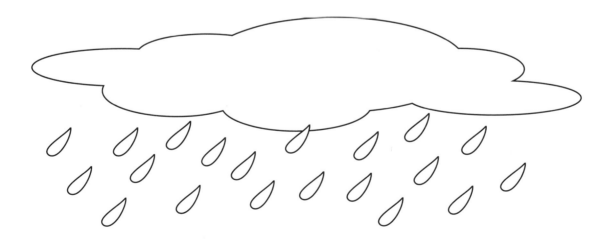

HOW STRESS FEELS

REPRESENTING STRESS WITH COLOR

OBJECTIVES   Students will:
- Identify areas of the body where stress reactions occur.
- Represent those reactions with color in creative drawings.
- Use the drawings to describe how stress feels.

MATERIALS   One copy of the experience sheet "The Color of Stress" for each student; crayons or colored marking pens

DIRECTIONS   Remind the students of discussions the group has had about stress, particularly those dealing with the feelings and physical sensations associated with stress. Ask a few questions to spark a quick review. Then state:

Our bodies can react strongly to stressful situations. Sometimes we don't realize what is causing those reactions. For example, you might get a headache or feel a little queasy after having an argument with a friend, or after being late to school because you missed the bus. If the reaction occurs a couple of hours later, it's easy to overlook the cause. That's just one reason why it is important to understand how you usually respond to stress.

Distribute the experience sheets and the drawing materials. As you go over the directions, emphasize the use of color. Urge the students to choose colors that represent their feelings. For example, what color comes to mind when they imagine feeling irritable, nervous, excited, or scared? Encourage the students to be as creative as possible and remind them that they all react to stress, but each in a different way.

Ask volunteers to show their completed drawings to the rest of the class and talk about what each rendering suggests and represents.

DISCUSSION QUESTIONS
1. What is the strongest reaction you have to stress?
2. What color did you use to represent that reaction?
3. What is the most unpleasant reaction you have to stress?
4. How did you represent that reaction?
5. Where in our bodies are strong and unpleasant reactions usually located?
6. What do you usually do when you have feelings like these?

THE COLOR OF STRESS
EXPERIENCE SHEET

Your body sends out signals when you experience stress. Sometimes the signals are very strong, such as when a loud crash makes you jump and your heart starts racing. Other times the signals are weak, such as when you feel a bit nervous before a quiz.

Use the picture below to mark the locations where you notice stress signals.

1. Draw an X on each part of the body where you feel stress. You may draw one X or several. Think about *how*

2. your body feels in each location you have marked.
   Choose a different color

3. to·represent each feeling or sensation.
   Use that color to fill

4. in the area where the reaction occurs.

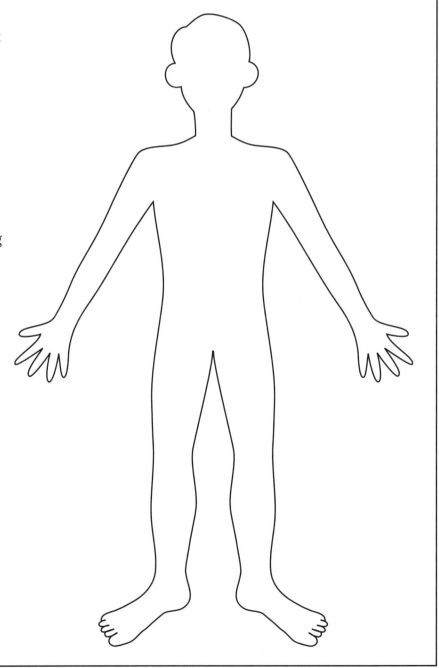

Less Student Stress, More School Success

IDENTIFYING LIFE STRESSORS
SELF-ASSESSMENT AND DISCUSSION

OBJECTIVES   Students will:
- Describe the "fight or flight" response in their own words.
- Identify specific things that cause stress in their lives.
- Name activities that tend to reduce stress.

MATERIALS   One copy of the experience sheet "Where Does Stress Come From?" for lower-grade students; one copy of the experience sheet "What Causes Stress in Your Life?" for upper-grade students

DIRECTIONS   Explain to the students that what we call stress, and the feelings that accompany stress, are not only natural and normal, they have been experienced by every human being who has ever lived. State:

Our earliest ancestors, the hunters and gatherers who lived long ago, evolved a very effective response to threats from predatory animals and other dangers. We call it the "fight or flight" response, because it helped them get ready to either stand their ground and fight an attacker, or try to escape. When your heart pounds and your muscles get tense, when your eyes widen and your fists clench, you are experiencing almost exactly the same physical response. But, instead of worrying about hungry lions, you worry about tests, and grades, and peer pressure, and a busy schedule that sometimes leaves you exhausted. Your bloodstream is flooded with the same chemical brew that helped your ancestors survive terrible threats to their safety, but you don't really need all those chemicals. In fact, they can end up damaging your health. That is why it is so important to learn to manage stress. When you know how to calm down and relax, you can slow or stop the flow of chemicals before they do any damage.

Point out that the first step to managing stress is to understand what causes the stress (fight or flight) response. Tell the students that they are going to complete a short self-assessment in order to identify sources of stress in their own lives.

Distribute the experience sheets and go over the directions. If you are working with lower-grade students, consider demonstrating the process. Allow about 10 minutes for completion.

Read through the stress factors listed on the experience sheet, asking for a show of hands from the students who marked each item. After polling an item, ask volunteers to elaborate on their individual experiences. Make notes on the board to keep track of the most common sources of stress.

Next, talk to the students about the need to take breaks when they feel stressed. Explain that a break is anything that helps them relax and gets their mind off tough issues. Ask the students to describe the stress breaks they listed on their experience sheets. Write their ideas on the board under the heading "Stress Breaks." Then brainstorm additional strategies, including:

- Jog or walk
- Listen to music
- Spend time with your pet
- Work on a hobby
- Play a game
- Browse the Internet
- Watch TV or a movie
- Practice a musical instrument
- Dance
- Play outdoors
- Talk with a relative or friend
- Make a plan to solve the stressful problem

Emphasize that stress breaks give the students time to recover from the fight-or-flight response, so that their bodies don't continue to produce potentially damaging chemicals, and that this is the primary goal of all stress-management strategies.

DISCUSSION QUESTIONS

1. What is meant by the words *fight-or-flight response*?
2. What is the fight-or-flight response designed to accomplish?
3. Why is the same event stressful for one person, but not stressful for another?
4. What things do most of us in this group find stressful?
5. How does your body feel when you are stressed?
6. Why is it important to relieve stress? What can happen if we don't?

Less Student Stress, More School Success

WHERE DOES STRESS COME FROM?
EXPERIENCE SHEET

Read the list below. Put a check mark (✓) beside any item that has happened to you. Put the check mark in the "B" column if the experience was bad. Put the check mark in the "G" column if the experience was good.

B	G	My stress comes from…
_____	_____	Trying to feel accepted
_____	_____	Arguing with my parents
_____	_____	Doing things I shouldn't because of peer pressure
_____	_____	Trying to make new friends
_____	_____	Worrying about my appearance
_____	_____	Feeling sad over the death of a pet
_____	_____	Feeling left out
_____	_____	Not having enough money
_____	_____	The death of a family member
_____	_____	Fighting with my brother or sister
_____	_____	My grade on a test
_____	_____	Arguing with or losing a friend
_____	_____	My ability in sports
_____	_____	Responsibilities or chores at home
_____	_____	Having no one to talk to
_____	_____	Death of a friend or classmate
_____	_____	Changing schools
_____	_____	Worrying about my safety
_____	_____	The separation or divorce of my parents
_____	_____	Grades on my report card
_____	_____	Thinking about vacation
_____	_____	Moving to a new neighborhood
_____	_____	Trying to please my parents

Take a Stress Break

Two things I do to feel better when I am stressed:

1. _____

2. _____

WHAT CAUSES STRESS IN YOUR LIFE?
EXPERIENCE SHEET

Read through the list. When you come to an area where you experience stress, write a short description of the thing that causes the stress. Remember two things:

1. A "change" in something can mean either more of it, or less of it.
2. Both positive events and negative events can cause stress.

HEALTH

- Personal injury or illness _____
- Change in a family member's health _____
- Change in personal-care habits _____
- Change in sleep patterns _____
- Change in eating habits _____
- Change in exercise habits _____
- Other _____

FRIENDS

- Problems with friend(s) _____
- Friend moving away _____
- Problems with boyfriend/girlfriend _____
- New friendship(s) _____
- New boyfriend/girlfriend _____
- Other _____

HOME

- Change of address _____
- Money problems at home _____
- Pregnancy or new child in family _____
- Change in living conditions _____
- Change in home responsibilities _____
- Brother/sister leaving home _____
- Trouble with parent(s) _____
- Parents separating/divorcing _____
- Other _____

 Less Student Stress, More School Success

EXCITEMENT/ANTICIPATION

- Outstanding personal achievement _____
- Holiday season _____
- Vacation _____
- Other _____

SCHOOL

- Starting new classes _____
- Change in study hours or conditions _____
- Change of school _____
- Trouble with teacher(s) _____
- New teacher(s) _____
- Exams/tests _____
- Report card _____
- Other _____

ACTIVITIES

- Change in number of family gatherings _____
- Change in leisure hours/habits _____
- Change in religious activities _____
- Change in social activities _____
- Other _____

DELINQUENCY

- Expelled or suspended from school _____
- Problems with alcohol/other drugs _____
- Trouble with law _____
- Other _____

DEATH

- Death of a family member _____
- Death of a friend _____
- Death of a pet _____
- Other _____

TAKE A STRESS BREAK

Three things I have done to relieve feelings of stress:

1. _____
2. _____
3. _____

Identifying Stressors   ©2010 by PRO-ED, Inc.   37

THE HEAVY WEIGHT OF STRESS
EXPERIENCE SHEET AND DISCUSSION

OBJECTIVES Students will:
- Understand stress and how it affects daily life.
- Describe how positive as well as negative events lead to stress.
- Identify individual stressors.

MATERIALS One copy of the experience sheet "Boulders in My Backpack" for each student

DIRECTIONS Spend a few minutes discussing the concept of stress — what it is, what it feels like, and how it interferes with daily life. State:

Stress is the general feeling of discomfort you experience when one or more responsibilities, problems, important events, worries, or life changes are weighing on your mind, demanding attention and energy. The things that cause stress are often referred to as stressors, and the more you are dealing with, the heavier the load. Imagine adding a rock to your backpack for every stressor in your day. Worried about a test? Add a rock. Have an argument with a friend? Add a rock. Big game this afternoon? Add a rock. Trouble with grades? Add a rock. Excited about a big event? Add a rock. Pretty soon it feels as though your backpack is bulging with boulders.

Ask the students to describe how stress makes them feel. As they share, write key words and phrases on the chalkboard. Common responses include: tense, tired, confused, drained, depressed, shaky, unable to concentrate, frustrated, exhausted, worthless.

Using age-appropriate vocabulary, paraphrase the following points about stress. Record notes on the board under these headings:

Negatives
- Worrying about stress won't make it go away.
- You can't outsmart stress.
- Good things cause stress, too.
- Stress can lower your resistance to illness.

Positives
- Understanding stress can help you manage it.
- You can learn to head off stress if you know where it comes from.
- Adequate rest and healthy eating can help you cope with stress.
- You can learn stress-reduction techniques.

Distribute the experience sheets and go over the directions. Give the students a few minutes to complete the sheet. When they have finished, go through the items with the entire group, asking for a show of hands to see how the items were rated. Ask volunteers to explain their ratings. Focus on both positive and negative feelings. Generate discussion throughout this process.

DISCUSSION QUESTIONS

1. How does being excited about something cause stress?
2. How does wanting to perform well cause stress?
3. What did you learn from rating different stressors?
4. How will this information help you manage your own stress levels?
5. How does stress affect our classroom?

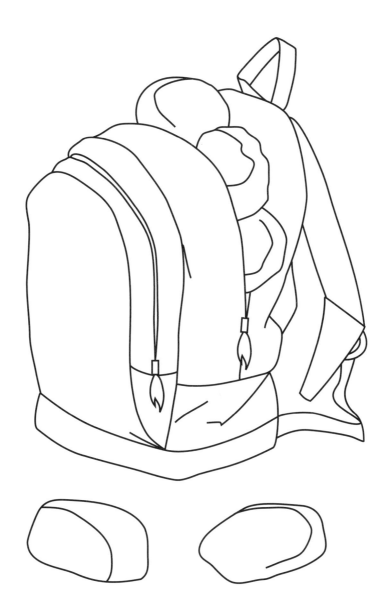

BOULDERS IN MY BACKPACK
EXPERIENCE SHEET

What if every stressor was represented by a rock in your backpack? The weight of all those rocks could get pretty heavy by the end of the day. Even if everything that happened was "good," some of it would still be stressful.

How you react determines whether something is stressful or not. For example, being called on in class is probably OK when you know the right answer. But it can be embarrassing when you don't. And the excitement of being invited to a party can be just as stressful as the disappointment of not being invited.

Decide how much stress you would feel in each of these situations. Draw an X on the scale from 1 (no stress) to 5 (very stressful).

Not Stressful .... Very Stressful

	1	2	3	4	5
1. Holding a snake	___	___	___	___	___
2. A photo of a snake	___	___	___	___	___
3. A school holiday	___	___	___	___	___
4. Getting an *A* on a test	___	___	___	___	___
5. Getting a *D* on your report card	___	___	___	___	___
6. Math class	___	___	___	___	___
7. Choosing teams in PE	___	___	___	___	___
8. The first day of school	___	___	___	___	___
9. The last day of school	___	___	___	___	___
10. A surprise quiz	___	___	___	___	___
11. Arguing with a friend	___	___	___	___	___
12. Making a new friend	___	___	___	___	___
13. Being late for school	___	___	___	___	___
14. Test-taking	___	___	___	___	___
15. Your birthday	___	___	___	___	___
16. Strange noises in the night	___	___	___	___	___
17. Being alone in the dark	___	___	___	___	___
18. Recess	___	___	___	___	___
19. Losing a game	___	___	___	___	___
20. Being invited to a party	___	___	___	___	___
21. The sound of a gun shot	___	___	___	___	___
22. Being the center of attention	___	___	___	___	___
23. A large barking dog	___	___	___	___	___
24. Overhearing gossip about yourself	___	___	___	___	___
25. Not being invited to a party	___	___	___	___	___

 Less Student Stress, More School Success

THE UPS AND DOWNS OF STRESS
LINKING EVENTS TO EMOTIONS

OBJECTIVES   Students will:
- Monitor their emotions for an entire day and evening.
- Link emotional changes to events and conditions throughout the day.
- Compute an average emotional level for the day.

MATERIALS   One or more copies of the experience sheet "The Ups and Downs of My Day" for each student (see directions)

DIRECTIONS   Begin by discussing the connection between emotions and stressful events. Explain that one good way to identify stressors is to pay attention to feelings. When we feel uncomfortable, nervous, or tense, chances are we are reacting to one or more stressful events or conditions. State:

For example, maybe you find yourself feeling edgy all afternoon. When you think back, you realize that, during lunch, you said something that seemed to upset your best friend. Without realizing it, you've been worried ever since. Or maybe you have a dental appointment after school, and feel more and more tense as the time draws near.

Explain that some events and emotions, like having a fight or feeling angry, can cause a person's emotions to suddenly drop into the basement. Other events and emotions can cause them to go sky-high. For example, laughter can sometimes raise our spirits very quickly.

Tell the students that they will have an opportunity to track their emotions and the events or conditions that influence them. Give each student one experience sheet and go over the directions carefully. Demonstrate the process by filling out an experience sheet yourself based on a previous day in your own life. Plot your emotions, write down what caused them and, when you are finished, compute your average emotional level for the entire day.

Identifying Stressors

Assign a specific day for completion of the experience sheet. On the following day, have the students share their finished sheets with a partner. Then bring the entire group together and ask volunteers to talk about what they learned. Facilitate discussion.

If you decide to repeat the exercise, distribute additional experience sheets.

DISCUSSION QUESTIONS
1. How much did your emotions change throughout the day?
2. What caused your biggest emotional drop?
3. What caused your biggest emotional spike?
4. How hard was it to figure out what caused your feelings to rise or fall?
5. What did you learn from this exercise that will help you to better manage stress?

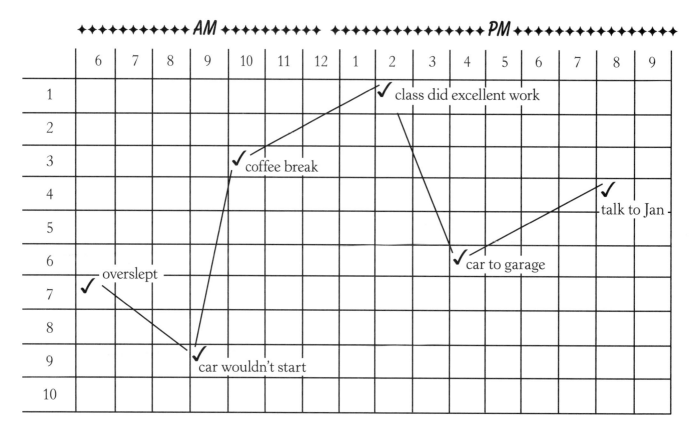

Finding an average:
add check marks 7 + 9 + 3 + 1 + 6 + 4 = 30; 30 ÷ 6 entries = 5 average

THE UPS AND DOWNS OF MY DAY
EXPERIENCE SHEET

Use this page to chart the ups and downs of your feelings for one whole day and evening. The scale on the left represents your feelings. It goes from very low (0) to very high (10).

DIRECTIONS

1. Mark your feeling level several times during the day.
2. Draw a line connecting one point to the next.
3. Write a few words about what caused your feelings to change.
4. At the end of the day, figure out the average of your feelings throughout the day.

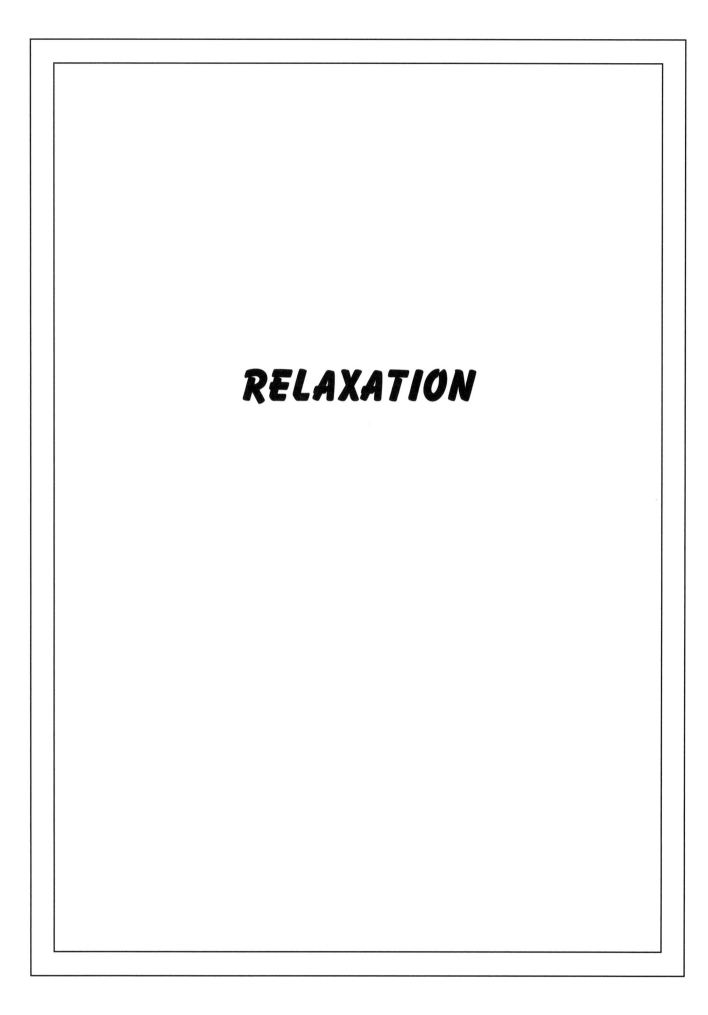

RELAXATION

DIFFUSING STRESS

EXPERIENCE SHEET AND DISCUSSION

OBJECTIVES
Students will:
- Review and discuss a variety of stress-reduction techniques.
- Identify new techniques that they would like to try.

MATERIALS
One copy of the experience sheet "Comfort Yourself!" for lower-grade students; one copy of the experience sheet "Soothing Solutions" for upper-grade students

DIRECTIONS
Give each student a copy of the appropriate experience sheet.

Read through the list of suggestions with the students, focusing briefly on one technique at a time. Ask for a show of hands from students who have tried the technique. Then ask for a show of hands from students who would *like* to try it.
Direct the students who have tried the technique to write a plus (+) mark next to the item, and the students who would like to try it to put a check (✓) mark beside the item.

As you review each strategy, discuss the types of situations in which it would work best. Ask students who have tried the technique to describe how well it worked. When the students mention additional techniques, write them on the board.

Elaborate on the importance of diffusing stressful situations, and emphasize the wide range of strategies available.

DISCUSSION QUESTIONS
1. What can happen if you do nothing and the stress keeps building?
2. How does physical exercise help relieve stress?
3. When does talking with someone work best?
4. Have you ever gotten rid of stress by solving a problem?
5. What are some unhealthy ways to relieve stress?

COMFORT YOURSELF!
EXPERIENCE SHEET

Put a + next to suggestions for coping with stress that you have *already* tried.
Put a ✓ beside suggestions you think you might *like* to try.

____ Read a book.
____ Blow soap bubbles.
____ Sculpt modeling clay.
____ Color or draw a picture.
____ Sing songs.
____ Play your favorite game.
____ Help a friend with homework.
____ Call grandma and grandpa.
____ Work on a jigsaw puzzle.
____ Go for a jog or walk.
____ Play a computer game.
____ Build something.
____ Fix yourself some hot chocolate.
____ Play with your pet.
____ Listen to happy or relaxing music.
____ Go to a park and swing really high.
____ Watch a movie.
____ Close your eyes and breathe deeply.
____ Play an instrument.

 Less Student Stress, More School Success

SOOTHING SOLUTIONS
EXPERIENCE SHEET

Put a + next to suggestions for copying with stress that you have *already* tried.
Put a ✓ beside suggestions you think you might *like* to try.

_____ Read a story.
_____ Meditate.
_____ Go to the mall with a friend.
_____ Do some stretching.
_____ Talk with, text, or email a friend.
_____ Watch a video.
_____ Take a run or walk.
_____ Take a nap.
_____ Listen to your favorite music.
_____ Play with your pet.
_____ Take a warm bath.
_____ Help a friend with homework or a hobby.
_____ Play an instrument.
_____ Draw or paint a picture.
_____ Daydream.
_____ Join a pickup game.
_____ Skateboard or rollerblade.
_____ Play a video or computer game.
_____ Think about the good things in your life.
_____ Finish something you've been putting off.

HELPING FRIENDS DEAL WITH STRESS
EXPERIENCE SHEET AND DISCUSSION

OBJECTIVES   Students will:
- Name ways to recognize signs of stress in others.
- Describe specific ways of helping friends deal with stress.

MATERIALS   One copy of the experience sheet "10 Ways to Help a Friend in Distress" for each student

DIRECTIONS   Begin by asking the students: "Have you ever been around a friend who was stressed out?" Ask for a show of hands and comment on the number who respond (probably the majority). Then ask: "How did you know that your friend was stressed out?"

Call on volunteers to describe clues that led them to their conclusions. Try to cover such common symptoms as a flushed, worried, or tense appearance; erratic, sullen, or hyper behavior; angry outbursts; and acting distracted or withdrawn. In many cases, the friends may simply have *shared* that they were stressed out.

Ask for a show of hands from students who tried to help their stressed-out friends. Facilitate sharing and discussion about the methods they used. List ideas on the board.

Distribute the experience sheets and go over the directions. Give the students about five minutes to write down as many ideas as they can think of. Then have the students form groups of three. Tell them to share their lists in the group and then brainstorm additional ideas. Suggest that each person record all of the ideas generated by the group. Allow about 15 minutes for sharing and brainstorming.

Reconvene the class and ask one person from each group to read that group's list. Comment on specific ideas to generate discussion and jot new ideas on the board. If the following ideas are not mentioned, suggest them yourself.

- Be a good listener.
- Express sympathy; say you are sorry that your friend feels stressed.
- Offer to go for a walk or bike ride with your friend.
- Suggest a game to play together.
- Offer to help your friend think of a solution.
- Suggest an adult to talk to.
- Give your friend a shoulder massage.
- Phone or text your friend later to see how things are going.
- Offer to help your friend study (if the stress is related to tests/grades).
- Tell a trusted adult about your friend's distress. (Discuss when this is appropriate.)

DISCUSSION QUESTIONS

1. Of the ways you have tried, which worked best?
2. What's a good thing to do if you have only a few minutes, or seconds, to help?
3. Why is it good to follow up later with a phone call, to see how your friend is doing?
4. When should you absolutely tell an adult? When should you avoid telling an adult?
5. If you felt stressed, how would you want your friends to help?

List 10 things that you can say or do to help a friend who is stressed. Describe helpful actions. Write down helpful statements word-for-word, just as if you were saying them.

1. _____

_____

2. _____

_____

3. _____

_____

4. _____

_____

5. _____

_____

6. _____

_____

7. _____

_____

8. _____

_____

9. _____

_____

10. _____

_____

Less Student Stress, More School Success

STRESS HAS MANY HANDLES
INTERVIEWS AND DISCUSSION

OBJECTIVES

Students will:
- Interview adults and peers to learn how they manage stress.
- Describe and compare several stress-reduction strategies.

MATERIALS

One copy of the experience sheet "How Do You Handle Stress?" for lower-grade students; one copy of the experience sheet "Getting a Handle on Stress" for upper-grade students

DIRECTIONS

Begin by relating the following incident to the students (or substitute a similar story from your own experience). Tell the students to listen carefully.

Four members of a school debate team (two girls and two boys) are waiting backstage for a big competition to begin. With them are their coach and two parents. The team is competing for the state championship. By winning, they not only take home a shiny engraved trophy, they also earn a trip to the national competition in Washington DC. The auditorium is filling up with people. With each passing minute, the tension builds. One girl is sitting very still with her eyes closed, breathing deeply. The other girl is getting a shoulder massage from one of the parents. One of the boys is pacing back and forth from one end of the room to the other. The second boy is listening to music on his ipod and moving to the beat. The coach and the other parent are huddled together talking quietly.

When you have finished relating the story, ask the students to describe the different things that these seven people are doing to ease the stress of waiting. Include:

- Deep breathing
- Physical activity (pacing)
- Listening to music
- Massage
- Talking

Emphasize that every individual develops favorite ways of handling stress. Some of those ways are deliberate and helpful. Others are automatic and may be less helpful. For example, some people become chatterboxes under stress, annoying everyone around them. Others try to reduce stress by eating huge bags of potato chips. Neither of these methods is terribly helpful.

Tell the students that they are going to find out how different people handle stress and share what they learn with the class.

Distribute the experience sheets and go over the directions. Assign a completion date.

If time permits, have the students share their completed experience sheets in small groups before convening the total group. This will give everyone a chance to share at least once. In the large group, ask volunteers to describe the coping methods of one or two people they interviewed. Facilitate discussion, comparing methods and their effectiveness.

DISCUSSION QUESTIONS

1. Which of the methods described by your interviewees seemed to work best?
2. What are some of the reasons that methods fail?
3. Why is it good to learn more than one way of coping with stress?
4. Which of the methods we've talked about have you tried? How well did they work?
5. Which new methods would you like to try?

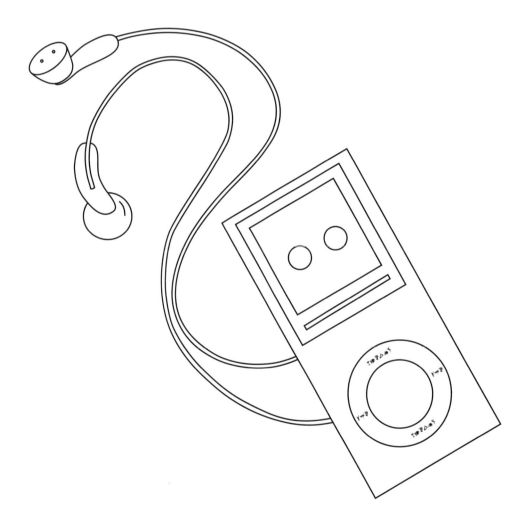

Less Student Stress, More School Success

 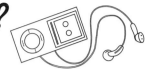

HOW DO YOU HANDLE STRESS?
EXPERIENCE SHEET

People handle stress in many different ways. Some of those ways work better than others. Learn how three different people cope with stress. Interview one parent, one other adult, and one friend. Write down their answers to the following questions:

PARENT

1. What do you *usually* do to cope with feelings of stress? _____

_____

2. Does this method relieve stress? ___Yes ___ No How quickly? _____

_____

3. Should I try this method? ___Yes ___ No Why or why not? _____

_____

4. What other methods do you use? _____

_____

ADULT

1. What do you *usually* do to cope with feelings of stress? _____

_____

2. Does this method relieve stress? ___Yes ___ No How quickly? _____

_____

3. Should I try this method? ___Yes ___ No Why or why not? _____

_____

4. What other methods do you use? _____

_____

FRIEND

1. What do you *usually* do to cope with feelings of stress? _____

_____

2. Does this method relieve stress? ___Yes ___ No How quickly? _____

_____

3. Should I try this method? ___Yes ___ No Why or why not? _____

_____

4. What other methods do you use? _____

_____

GETTING A HANDLE ON STRESS
EXPERIENCE SHEET

Stress doesn't play favorites. It affects everyone. We all learn ways of coping with stressful events and the uncomfortable feelings they cause. We do things to relax our bodies and distract our minds. Some ways of relieving stress work better than others.

Interview five different people to learn how they cope with stress. Interview three adults and two peers. You can choose from parents, grandparents, aunts, uncles, neighbors, teachers, coaches, friends, brothers, and sisters. Ask each person the following questions. Write their answers below.

1. What is the biggest source of stress in your life?
   Adult 1: _____
   Adult 2: _____
   Adult 3: _____
   Peer 1: _____
   Peer 2: _____

2. What is your "favorite" way of coping with stress?
   Adult 1: _____
   Adult 2: _____
   Adult 3: _____
   Peer 1: _____
   Peer 2: _____

3. Why do you use this method?
   Adult 1: _____
   _____
   Adult 2: _____
   _____
   Adult 3: _____
   _____
   Peer 1: _____
   _____
   Peer 2: _____
   _____

   Less Student Stress, More School Success

4. How well does this method work for you?

Adult 1: _____
_____

Adult 2: _____
_____

Adult 3: _____
_____

Peer 1: _____
_____

Peer 2: _____
_____

5. What other methods have you tried—or would you like to try?

Adult 1: _____
_____

Adult 2: _____
_____

Adult 3: _____
_____

Peer 1: _____
_____

Peer 2: _____
_____

LOL FOR HEALTH
DEMONSTRATIONS AND DISCUSSION

OBJECTIVES
Students will:
- Laugh.
- Describe how laughing makes them feel.
- Discuss the benefits of using laughter as a stress-reduction technique.

MATERIALS
None

DIRECTIONS
Write the heading "Laughter" on the board and introduce the activity by stating: "Today we're going to talk about laughter, the most powerful stress buster of them all. Better yet, in addition to *talking* about laughter, we are going to laugh."

Ask for a show of hands from students who have laughed at least once that day. Acknowledge the number, whether many or few. Then, one at a time, write the following synonyms on the board, and ask, "Was it a _____?"

- Tee-hee
- Snicker
- Giggle
- Chortle
- Chuckle
- Yuk
- Hoot
- Roar
- Howl
- Belly laugh
- Side-splitting crack up

While counting the hands for each type of laughter, ask various students to demonstrate how each one looks and sounds. For example, say, "Show us what a 'snicker' looks like, Shelly," or "Show us how a chortle is different from a chuckle, Ruben."

Get everyone involved in mimicking the various demonstrations. Ham it up, asking the demonstrator (and the class), "Is this right?" and "Does Mark have it, or is that more of a belly laugh?"

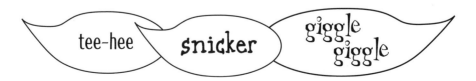

When the demonstrations are finished and the class has quieted down, ask the students how they feel. Facilitate a discussion about the effects of laughter. Point out that laughter is not only fun, it is healthy. It reduces stress quickly and effectively while at the same time increasing:

- Relaxation
- Blood flow to the brain and body
- Alertness and productivity
- Positive feelings
- Ability to remember
- Creativity
- Ability to solve problems and resolve conflicts

Ask the students what makes them laugh. Call on volunteers to describe the things they find truly funny, such as particular TV shows, comedians, comic actors, cartoons, and funny friends and relatives. Expand the discussion to include the use of humor as a deliberate conflict-resolution strategy as well as a stress-reduction strategy.

DISCUSSION QUESTIONS

1. When have you used humor to help resolve a conflict? How well did it work?
2. Have you ever defused someone's anger by saying something funny? Tell us about it.
3. What can you do at home to trigger laughter when you are feeling stressed?
4. When you feel stressed at school, what can you do to lighten up?
5. What does it mean when someone says, "He has a good sense of humor"?
6. How can you develop a good sense of humor?

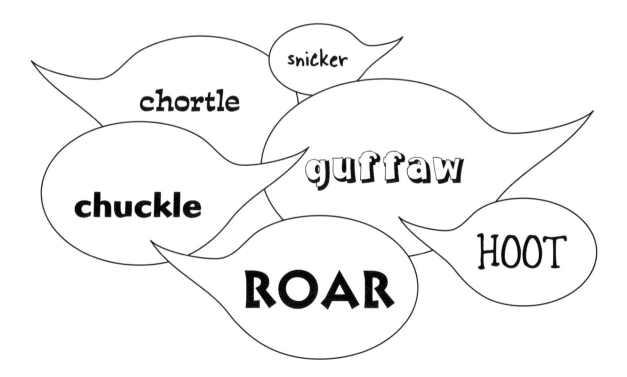

RELAX AND RECHARGE
EXPERIENCE SHEET AND DISCUSSION

OBJECTIVES   Students will:
- Recall and compare recent periods of stress and relaxation.
- Identify people and activities that help them relax.
- Discuss the importance of scheduling daily periods of relaxation.

MATERIALS   One copy of the experience sheet "Recharge Your Battery" for each student

DIRECTIONS   Ask for a show of hands from students who use an iPod or a cell phone. Talk about what happens when the battery gets low:

First, the user gets a warning. If they ignore the warning, pretty soon they get a more urgent warning. Buzzers go off and signals flash. Finally, when all the juice is gone, the battery goes dead and the device stops working.

Point out that our bodies are a bit like iPods and cell phones. If we go, go, go all the time and never stop to recharge, eventually we start getting warning signals—headaches, stomachaches, jangled nerves, short tempers, and crying jags. If we continue to ignore the warnings and push ourselves without recharging, we might even get seriously ill. At the very least our performance at school and in all those activities that keep us so busy will suffer.

Distribute the experience sheets and go over the directions. Explain that the sheet asks the students to mentally review the past few days and compare the time spent relaxing to the time spent feeling stressed.

In a follow-up discussion, focus on the need to deliberately schedule one or more periods of relaxation into every busy day. Refer to the battery analogy periodically to concretize the notion of recharging.

DISCUSSION QUESTIONS
1. Which people and activities help you relax?
2. What kinds of situations tend to produce stress?
3. How satisfied are you with the amount of relaxation you get in a day?
4. How difficult is it for you to schedule periods of relaxation?
5. What changes could you make in your schedule to leave more time for relaxation?

RECHARGE YOUR BATTERY
EXPERIENCE SHEET

Stress can wear you down. When it does, you need to make time to relax. Just like the battery on your iPod or cell phone, you need to recharge. Think back over the last few days. Try to remember when you felt relaxed and when you felt stressed. Recall exactly what was happening—whom you were with and what you were doing.

1. Focus on the times when you felt completely relaxed. How did it feel? _____
_____

2. Focus on the times when you felt stressed. How did that feel? _____
_____

3. What thoughts did you have when you were relaxed? _____
_____

4. What thoughts did you have when you were stressed? _____
_____

5. Who were you with when you felt relaxed? _____
_____

6. What activities were you doing when you felt relaxed? _____
_____

7. Do you try to do something relaxing every day? ____ Yes ____ No

8. Would it help you to relax more often? ____ How? _____
_____

RELAXATION THREE WAYS

DEEP BREATHING, MEDITATION, AND MUSCLE RELAXATION

OBJECTIVES   Students will:
- Learn and practice three relaxation techniques.
- Understand the purpose of each technique.
- Compare the relative benefits of the three techniques.

MATERIALS   Reasonable space and moveable chairs; optional soft instrumental music

DIRECTIONS   The essence of stress reduction is relaxation. You can repeatedly urge mindfulness and relaxation, explaining in detail their value, but until you actually *teach* and *routinely practice* methods to accomplish these objectives — prior to tests, following breaks, as transitions from active to quiet tasks — nothing much will change.

Below are three distinct methods of achieving relaxation. Each is simple, easy to learn, and effective. The key to success is repetition. Have your students practice one or more of these exercises regularly. Make relaxation part of their routine.

Deep Breathing

The simplest, most direct route to relaxation is that of deep breathing. Explain to the students that when they are tense, nervous, angry, or excited, their breathing becomes more rapid. Deliberately slowing and controlling the depth and rate of their breathing can help them to calm down and feel more relaxed.

Read the directions slowly, progressing from chest to abdominal (belly) breathing and then combining the movements in one slow, continuous four-count exercise.

Chest-breathing

1. Sit in a comfortable position and close your eyes.
2. Inhale and exhale deeply through your nose three times.
3. Place your left hand on your stomach, just below your ribs. Place your right hand on your chest.
4. Breathe normally and notice where your breath is coming from.
5. Now take a long, slow, deep breath into your chest. Your right hand will rise while your left hand remains fairly still.
6. Pause briefly, keeping your chest full, then exhale slowly through your nose.
7. Repeat this "chest breathing" three times.
8. Breathe in, hold, release... breathe in, hold, release... breathe in, hold, release.
9. Breathe normally.

Belly-breathing

1. Now, take a long, slow deep breath into your stomach. Your left hand will rise, while your right hand remains fairly still.
2. Pause briefly, feeling your stomach muscles push up, then exhale slowly through your nose.
3. Repeat this "belly breathing" three times.
4. Breathe in, hold, release... breathe in, hold, release... breathe in, hold, release.
5. Breathe normally.

Combined chest-belly breathing

1. Count one: breathe into your belly (left hand rises)
2. Count two: breathe into your chest (right hand rises)
3. Count three: Exhale from your belly (left hand lowers)
4. Count four: Exhale from your chest (right hand lowers)
5. Pause.
6. Repeat: one... two... three... four...
7. Continue for 2-3 minutes.

5-Minute Meditation

Explain to the students that the purpose of meditation is to relax the body and quiet the mind. Point out that our bodies are usually active and moving. Even while sitting, we tend to shift, turn, and twitch. Similarly, our minds never stop producing thoughts, not even during sleep. By sitting quietly for a few minutes while breathing naturally and focusing all of our attention on a particular sound, we can calm both mind and body.

In this exercise the students will focus on the sound of their own voice counting from one to four. Have the students move their chairs to create maximum distance from one another. If possible, they should face blank walls, or at least face away from other students. A circle, with everyone turned to face out, works well. Tell the students to count very quietly, just above a whisper.

Slowly read these directions:

1. Sit straight in your chair. Fold your hands in your lap or rest them on your thighs.
2. Look down slightly with your eyes, keeping your head straight.
3. Sit quietly and try not to move. Breathe naturally.

Pause briefly, then continue...

4. Focus your attention on your breathing.
5. Silently count "one" as you inhale. Count "two" as you exhale. Count "three" as you inhale. Count "four" as you exhale.
6. Continue breathing in and out with each count up to ten.
7. Start over, breathing and counting up to ten.
8. Concentrate on the sound of your own voice counting. If other thoughts enter your mind, that's okay. Just let them pass and go back to focusing on your voice.
9. Continue for 5 minutes.

Progressive Muscle Relaxation

One of the best ways to differentiate a tense muscle from a relaxed one, thereby guaranteeing relaxation, is to first exaggerate the tension. Progressive muscle relaxation helps students feel the difference by tensing and relaxing one muscle group at a time, from toe to head. As you read the directions, exaggerate your inflexion to convey the alternate sensations of tension and relaxation. Play the role of coach.

1. Sit or lie in a comfortable position with your eyes closed. Breathe naturally.
2. Think about each set of muscles as I tell you to tense and hold for 5 seconds. Try to move only the muscles I tell you to move, keeping the rest of your body still. Notice how it feels. Then notice the difference when I tell you to relax those muscles.
3. Tense your toes by flexing them as though you were standing on tiptoe. Hold. Relax.
4. Flex your ankles and move them around in circles. Flex again. Hold. Relax.
5. Tense and stretch your calf muscles by pushing hard with your heels. Hold. Relax.
6. Tense the large muscles in your thighs. Hold. Relax.
7. Tense your hip and buttocks muscles. Feel your hips lift. Hold. Relax.
8. Tense your abdominal muscles. Feel them tighten. Hold. Relax.
9. Tense your stomach muscles. Suck them in as tightly as you can. Hold. Relax.
10. Make tight fists with your fingers. Tighter. Hold. Relax.
11. Flex your wrists. Make circles with your wrists. Flex again. Hold. Relax.
12. Tense the muscles in your arms. Make your arms as stiff as boards. Hold. Relax.
13. Tense your shoulder muscles. Hunch your shoulders up to your ears. Hold. Relax.
14. Tense your neck by touching your chin to your collarbone. Hold. Relax.
15. Turn your neck as far as it will go to the right. Hold. Relax.
16. Turn your neck as far as it will go to the left. Hold. Relax.
17. Scrunch all the muscles of your face as tightly as you can. Hold. Relax.
18. Now tense your whole body, starting with your toes all the way up to your face. Hold. Relax.

DISCUSSION QUESTIONS

1. Which of the three relaxation exercises did you like best? Why?
2. Which exercise was most effective in helping you to relax?
3. Which exercise are you most apt to use on your own?
4. During the meditation, how difficult was it to concentrate on counting?
5. During the muscle relaxation exercise, where did you feel the most tension?
6. During what part of your day are you usually very relaxed? When are you usually very tense?
7. Which of these techniques could you use to relax during the tense part of your day?

EXTENSION

Prior to teaching the deep breathing technique to young children, have them get the feel of deep breathing by blowing bubbles. Bubble-blowing enlists many of the same facial muscles and requires nearly identical breath control. The students learn that slow, steady breathing produces streams of bubbles, while hard and soft blowing does not.

CALMING NOTES

RELAXATION TO MUSIC

OBJECTIVES
Students will:
- Relax to quiet music.
- Describe how music can be used to reduce stress.

MATERIALS
Relaxing instrumental music (composers/performers such as Vivaldi, Pachelbel, Debussy, Kitaro, and Yanni)

DIRECTIONS
Talk with the students about using music to promote relaxation and stress reduction. Acknowledge that while everyone has particular tastes in music, when the goal is to relax, not just any music will do. Fast, rhythmic music energizes us and makes us want to move. Lyrics inspire us to sing along. So when we want to relax our minds and bodies, it's better to choose quiet music with a slow beat and no vocals.

Play excerpts from two or three selections of relaxing music. Suggest that the students close their eyes while they listen. Then ask the students what they think of the music. Tell them a little about the composer and/or performer.

Next, play a longer selection while you lead the students in a simple guided relaxation. Pause for a few moments between sentences as you softly repeat these directions:

Settle back in a comfortable position and close your eyes. Mentally scan your body. Notice which muscles are tense and which are relaxed, and where you feel pain. Be aware of your mood. Now, focus all of your attention on the music. When unrelated thoughts cross your mind, just let them pass. Allow the music to relax the parts of your body that feel tense. Complete relaxation is your goal. Say to yourself, "Relax... relax... relax..."

When the music ends, tell the students to remain where they are, with their eyes closed. After a full minute, state:

Without opening your eyes, scan your body again. Be aware of how it feels. Does your body feel different than it did before you started? Is there any difference in your mood?

Have the students open their eyes. Facilitate a brief discussion about the experience.

DISCUSSION QUESTIONS
1. What differences do you notice in your body since doing the exercise?
2. How has your mood changed?
3. How difficult was it to concentrate on the music?
4. Do you relax to music at home? What kind of music?
5. What have you learned today about reducing stress?

SOFT EYES

PRACTICE IN RELAXED ALERTNESS

OBJECTIVES　　Students will:
- Practice both focused vision and peripheral vision and describe the differences.
- Experiment with the use of peripheral vision to achieve relaxed alertness.
- Name circumstances where relaxed alertness is beneficial.

MATERIALS　　A solid red circle about 4 inches in diameter, hand drawn and colored on illustration board or plain white poster paper; tape; computers with Internet, encyclopedias, or health texts for the extension

DIRECTIONS　　Tape the red circle on a wall where all students can see it, about 45 degrees above eye level when seated. Tell the students to focus all their attention on the circle, seeing all the details, noticing light and dark spots and other variations. Tell them to stare intently, blinking as needed.

After 1 minute (time it) state:

Continue looking at the circle while you gradually relax the muscles of your eyes. You are still looking at the circle, but no longer staring. As your eyes relax, become aware of what is to the right and left of the circle, and what is above and below the circle. Hold your arms out and move them back and forth at shoulder level, wiggling your fingers. Notice where the finger movement disappears from your field of vision. Remember, you are still looking at the circle, but your eyes are relaxed.

After 1 minute (time it), have the students repeat the exercise twice more, staring first, then relaxing into peripheral vision.

After three rounds of the exercise, ask volunteers to describe what they experienced. Discuss the different sensations and feelings produced by the two types of vision, writing key descriptors on the board.

Explain to the students that focused vision, also called *foveal* vision, emanates from the *fovea*, a small depression in the retina of the eye where visual acuity is highest. The center of a person's field of vision is focused in this area, where the cones of the retina are highly concentrated. A cone is a light sensitive cell that is responsible for sharpness and color perception. When the students stared intently at the circle, they were using primarily foveal vision.

When they relaxed their eyes, they were using a different kind of cell, called a rod. Rods allow them to see what is happening around them. This type of vision is usually called *peripheral*. Rods are responsible for the ability to see in poor light, which we often refer to as *night vision*.

Point out that foveal vision helps us concentrate on whatever we're involved in, whether it's a book, a TV program, a computer screen, a test, or a conversation. Because foveal vision involves intense concentration, it is also associated with higher levels of stress. Peripheral vision allows us to be aware of what's going on around us. For example, during a fast game of soccer, foveal vision keeps us focused on the position and direction of the ball, while peripheral vision informs us of the movements, positions and intentions of other players. Peripheral vision is associated with relaxation. Skilled soccer players employ both types of vision at the same time. As a result, they are alert and relaxed at the same time. Relaxed alertness is the optimal state for all kinds of activities, not just sports. It is an ideal for learning. State:

Peripheral awareness is called "soft eyes" by Native Americans and other aboriginal groups. The technique enables hunters to walk easily in the dark. It reduces their fear response (stress) and allows them to see the movements of animals. Once you get the feel of it, you can relax into peripheral vision whenever you want to. It's easy and it quickly relieves stress.

Conclude the activity by having the students practice "soft eyes" several times while focusing on other things in the room (clock, window, flag, picture, their neighbor). With each repetition, urge them to speed up the transition from foveal to peripheral vision.

DISCUSSION QUESTIONS

1. Did your breathing change when you switched from foveal to peripheral vision? How?
2. What happened to the muscles of your face and jaw?
3. Why would it be important to use "soft eyes" when skateboarding or riding a bike?
4. How would "soft eyes" help drivers?
5. What other activities would benefit from the use of "soft eyes?"

EXTENSION

Have the students research the mechanics of vision, in the process defining terms such as retina, rod, peripheral, cone and fovea. Have them locate and share diagrams of the eye showing all it's parts.

Adapted from an activity by Keith Ward, Ph.D.

TELL YOUR STORY

WRITING AND DISCUSSION

OBJECTIVES   Students will:
- Brainstorm common stressful and relaxing activities.
- Write short stories about stressful and relaxing events.
- Explain how they contribute to and control their own stress levels.

MATERIALS   Writing materials

DIRECTIONS   Write the headings "Stressful" and "Relaxing" on the board. Ask the students to brainstorm two lists of activities—things they commonly do in the course of a day. Jot down each idea under one of the headings, based on whether the students consider the activity stressful or relaxing. If they seem uncertain, or if you get mixed opinions, facilitate discussion to further clarify the item.

After you have listed as many activities as the students can generate, explain the writing assignment. Ask the students to each write two short stories, one story about the most stressful day they can remember having, and the other about a wonderfully relaxing day. Stipulate a maximum length for the stories, e.g., one page each.

Have the students share their completed stories in small groups of three to five. Tell them to take turns reading their "stressful" stories first. Then have them read their "relaxing" stories. Separate the two rounds of sharing with a large-group discussion. Use the discussion questions below and ask follow-up questions of your own.

DISCUSSION QUESTIONS
1. What were some of the stressful events you shared in your group?
2. What did your stressful stories have in common?
3. Which, if any, stressful stories had happy endings? What made them happy?
4. What did you do to contribute to the stress in your own story?
5. What could you have done differently to lessen the stress?
6. What were some of the relaxing events you shared?
7. What did your relaxing stories have in common?
8. What, if anything, did you do to create your own relaxation?
9. What new ideas did you hear for reducing stress?
10. Which type of story was easier to think of and write? Why?

EXTENSION   To extend the writing experience, have the students return to small groups and help each other edit and rewrite one or more of their stories. Integrate the steps in this activity with practices from your standard writing program.

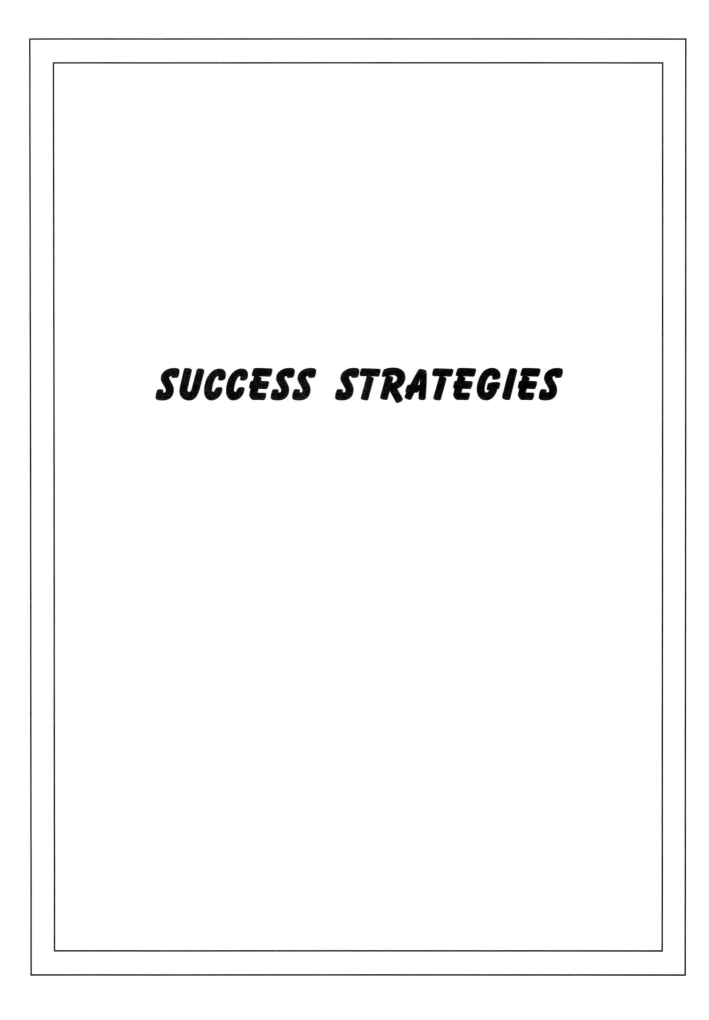

SUCCESS STRATEGIES

AFFIRMATION BREAK

A SIMPLE VISUALIZATION

OBJECTIVES

Students will:
- Experience a period of quiet and relaxation.
- Repeat positive affirmations in a controlled setting.

MATERIALS

None

DIRECTIONS

Have the students close their eyes and picture themselves in a peaceful scene, such as a garden, beach, park, mountain oasis, or quiet room. Read the following directions aloud. If you wish, modify the script to include statements that are more appropriate or relevant to your group.

Sit in a comfortable position and relax. (Pause) Close your eyes and take a deep breath. (Pause) Tell yourself to relax completely. (Pause) Listen to your breathing. (Pause) Allow your body to rest and completely relax. (Pause) Pay attention to your breathing. (Pause) Take a deep breath, hold it, and let it out slowly. (Pause) Now, I'm going to make several statements. Repeat each one silently to yourself. "I am relaxed and comfortable." (Pause) "I feel happy and peaceful." (Pause) "My body is completely relaxed." (Pause) "I am healthy and strong…" (Pause) "…and totally relaxed." (Pause) "I take good care of myself." (Pause) "I am a special person in my family." (Pause) Now, think of something that is important to you. For example, an important activity or item that you want to do or have. Send yourself a positive message about this important thing. (Pause) Repeat the message. (Pause) Now, think of a different event, achievement or item. Send yourself a positive message about that one, too. (Pause) Repeat the message. (Pause) Accept that these messages are absolutely true. (Pause) Take a deep breath and let it out slowly. (Pause) Take another breath. (Pause) When you are ready, open your eyes and stretch your body gently.

DISCUSSION QUESTIONS

1. How well were you able to relax and concentrate on the affirmations?
2. Do you feel more relaxed now than you did before the activity?
3. Why is it important to say positive things to ourselves?
4. When during the day would it help to close your eyes and give yourself one or more positive messages? Before a test? Before a game? When you feel tense or upset?
5. Have you tried doing affirmations on your own? What was the result?

HOW GOALS REDUCE STRESS
EXPERIENCE SHEET AND DISCUSSION

OBJECTIVES   Students will:
- Explain how having goals helps reduce stress.
- Discuss the importance of goals.
- Practice writing long and short-term goals.

MATERIALS   One copy of the experience sheet "Seven Goals" for each student

DIRECTIONS   Begin by discussing the connection between goal setting and stress reduction. Explain that having clear goals makes it much easier to decide how to use time wisely. And using time wisely (time management) is one of the very best ways of reducing or preventing stress.

Ask two or three volunteers to describe a personal or school-related goal. If the students have trouble thinking of goals, help them along by mentioning several categories of goals, including education, family, extracurricular, career and health/fitness (write these on the board). Students who can answer the frequently-asked question, "What do you want to do when you grow up?" are stating a career goal. Students who want to master a sport, or make a team, have an extracurricular goal (or it might be considered a health/fitness goal).

When you are sure that the students understand the concepts of goals and goal setting, distribute the experience sheets and go over the directions, explaining that they are going to practice writing goals.

Direct the students to write two long-term goals (to be accomplished within one year), two short term (to be accomplished within the next month) and one immediate goal (to be accomplished within one or two days). Give some examples. If you are working with lower-grade students, keep the goals school related. If you are working with upper-grade students, explain that the goals can be related to any part of their lives (school, family, extracurricular, career, health/fitness).

Have upper-grade students go back over their lists and assign an A, B, or C priority to each goal. The A's are the most important goals. The B's are also important, but less so than the A's. B's can be temporarily postponed. The C's are the least important goals and can be put off for as long as necessary. Encourage the students to develop plans, timelines, and to-do lists for their "A" goals. Urge them to make a conscious effort to regularly schedule time to work on them.

DISCUSSION QUESTIONS

1. What is one goal that you recently accomplished?
2. How did you feel when you accomplished your goal?
3. What is a goal that you are working on now?
4. How much time do you spend working on your goal?
5. What happens when you fail to devote time to goals?
6. Why is it easier to attain goals that you set than it is to attain goals that someone else sets for you?

SEVEN GOALS
EXPERIENCE SHEET

A goal in life is very much like a goal on the soccer field or basketball court. It is something that you want to accomplish. When you say, "I want to get an A on the test," you are stating a goal. When you say, "I plan to go to the game on Friday," you are stating another goal.

Write two long-term goals below. A long-term goal is something you plan to accomplish within one year.

1. _____
_____
2. _____
_____

Write two short-term goals here. A short-term goal is something you plan to accomplish within the next month.

1. _____
_____
2. _____
_____

Write one immediate goal. An immediate goal is something you plan to accomplish within the next two days.

1. _____
_____

TIPS FOR WRITING GOALS

1. Write *your* goals, about things that *you* want (not what your teacher or parents want).

2. Choose goals that can be reached, not goals that are impossible to reach.

3. Make goals specific. Say *exactly* what you want in as much detail as possible.

 Less Student Stress, More School Success

WHO CAN HELP?

EXPERIENCE SHEET AND DISCUSSION
(LOWER GRADES)

OBJECTIVES

Students will:
- Identify sources of help and support for stressful times.
- Describe situations where help or adult intervention may be needed.

MATERIALS

One copy of the experience sheet "The Road to Help" for each student

DIRECTIONS

Initiate a discussion about stressful situations that demand help or intervention from others, particularly adults. Describe a few examples and ask the students to think of others, such as:

- Being bullied or harassed
- Falling behind in school
- Grieving the loss of a family member or close friend
- Abuse of any kind from anyone

Emphasize that the students do not have to deal with stressful situations and difficult problems alone. There are many people both able and willing to assist them when they need help.

Distribute the experience sheets and go over the directions. Give the students a few minutes to complete the sheet. Then discuss the results as a group.

DISCUSSION QUESTIONS

1. Which of the remaining words describe people that you could go to for help?
2. Why are some problems too big to handle alone?
3. What could happen if you didn't get help?
4. What can you do if you are fearful or shy about asking for help?
5. When have you asked for help and been glad you did?

 WHOOOoo **THE ROAD TO HELP** WHOOOoo **EXPERIENCE SHEET**

When you are upset or have a problem, share your feelings with someone you trust. It helps!

Follow these directions:

1. Draw a line through all the words that name an animal.
2. Draw a line through all the words that name a place.
3. Draw a line through all the words that name a number.
4. Draw a line through all the words that name a thing.
5. Draw a line through all the words that name a toy.
6. Look at what's left. Circle the words that name someone you could ask for help.

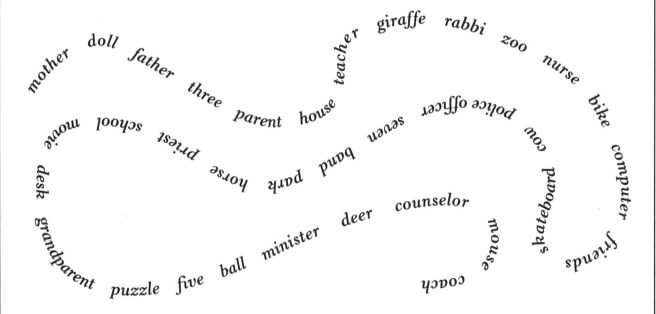

Your problems may seem unique, but they are not. Most people have dealt with similar problems. When you reach out for help, you can learn from the experience and ideas of others. Don't forget, adults were your age once.

Name three people who you can ask for help when you have a problem.

1.
2.
3.

Are you willing to ask these people for help?____ Yes ____ No

 Less Student Stress, More School Success

HELP WHEN YOU NEED IT

RESEARCH AND REPORTING
(UPPER GRADES)

OBJECTIVES   Students will:

Define emergency situations in which outside help may be needed.
Identify individuals and organizations that can provide help.
Research and record contact information for selected helpers.

MATERIALS   One copy of the HELP Register for each student; one 5x8 index card for each student

DIRECTIONS   nitiate a discussion about stressful situations that call for outside help. Talk about emergencies such as accidents, power failures, medical crises, illness, fires, and criminal acts. In addition, discuss the kinds of personal difficulties that might cause extreme loneliness, depression, helplessness, fear, or panic. Point out that in situations like these it is extremely important to know where to seek help.

Distribute the HELP Register and a 5x8 card to each student. Have the students write the following on their 5x8 cards:

Name of organization:
Address:
Phone:
Contact person:
Resources available:
Steps to follow to obtain resources:

Explain that each of the students will be responsible for obtaining and sharing information about one of the items listed on the HELP Register under the heading "Organizations." Explain that this work must be done outside of class. Assign a firm due date.

In addition, the students should ask a parent to help them complete the items under the heading "People." Because this information is personal and will vary from one student to the next, it will not be shared in class.

Divide the "Organizations" items evenly among the students. If two or more students are assigned the same item (this will happen in larger groups), try to arrange for them to investigate organizations in different parts of the community, particularly if the school serves a wide geographical area.

Tell the students to use the Internet and phone directories to obtain information. Urge those who don't have Internet access at home to use the school media center or community library. Encourage them to ask for assistance from staff, if needed.

At a follow-up session, have the students take turns sharing the information they obtained. Discuss the services provided by each resource organization and clarify the steps involved in securing those services. You may wish to spread this portion of the activity over several sessions. Instruct the students to record appropriate organization names and phone numbers on their own HELP Register.

When all of the information has been shared and the students have completed their HELP Registers, have one of the students collect the 5x8 cards and arrange them alphabetically in a card file that will remain available to the class. Encourage the students to display their HELP Registers in a prominent location at home, or keep them in a safe, accessible location.

DISCUSSION QUESTIONS

1. What questions should you ask to learn the correct procedure when calling a particular organization?
2. What should you do if you can't reach the person or organization you need?
3. When should you call the police?
4. When might you need to call Animal Control?
5. When was the last time you phoned someone for help? Who was it?

VARIATION

In place of index cards, provide 8-1/2 x 11 sheets pre-printed with the required information headings. Collect the sheets at the end of the activity, put them in protective clear plastic sheets and store them in a three-ring binder.

CLASS
HELP
REGISTER

HELP REGISTER

Complete this phone register and keep it in a prominent location. Get help quickly when you need it!

PEOPLE

Parents at work _____
Grandparents _____
Neighbor/Friend _____
Neighbor/Friend _____
Doctor _____
Dentist _____
Counselor/Therapist/Social Worker _____
Big Brother/Sister _____
Pastor/Rabbi/Other Clergy _____

ORGANIZATIONS

Schools _____
_____
_____
Emergency Fire or EMS _____
Non-emergency Fire or EMS _____
Police/Sheriff _____
_____
Poison Control _____
_____
Suicide Prevention _____
Crisis Center _____
_____
Hospital Emergency _____
_____
Domestic Violence Shelter _____
Legal Aid _____
Gas & Electric Company _____
Emergency Water & Sewer _____
Animal Control _____

POSITIVE PROGRAMMING
EXPERIENCE SHEET AND DISCUSSION

OBJECTIVES   Students will:
- Contrast negative with positive self-talk.
- Understand the benefits of positive affirmations.
- Write a positive affirmation.

MATERIALS   One copy of the experience sheet "Write Your Own Program" for each student

DIRECTIONS   Begin by asking the students to think about the way they talk to themselves about *themselves*. Have them imagine several scenarios: that they've done something embarrassing, or failed a test, or can't understand a math formula, or were left out of a group. Ask volunteers to tell the class what they would say or think to themselves in each situation. Typical self-deprecating responses are, "That was really dumb," "I'm such a loser," "I'll never get this stuff," and "Who needs those guys anyhow."

Point out that our tendency to put ourselves down is extremely strong. In order to overcome it, we need to deliberately replace negative statements with positive statements, called "affirmations."

Explain that an affirmation is a positive, supportive statement that "affirms" that you are smart, capable, successful, creative, well-liked, and all the other things you want to be. The logic behind affirmations goes something like this: since you probably talk to yourself anyway, and since your brain records whatever you tell it, you might as well say things that are helpful. If you say something often enough and with sufficient conviction, it becomes a well-worn path in your brain. So it creates; paths to success, not failure.

Tell the students that they are going to have an opportunity to practice writing and speaking affirmations, but first they need to learn the rules. Write the following guidelines on the board, discussing each one.

Affirmations are:

1. **Within your control**. Affirmations must be about something over which you have control. For example, saying "Sal likes me" won't work because you can't control Sal's brain, only your own.

2. **Positive**. Saying "I'm smart" is more effective than saying "I'm no dummy."

3. **Present tense**. Saying "I'm winning" is better than saying "I will win."

4. **Convey feeling**. Use words that express strong emotion and conviction.

5. **Realistic**. Don't affirm something so unlikely that you can't possibly achieve it.

Distribute the experience sheets. Ask several students to read aloud the example affirmations like they really believe them—with feeling. Then give the students a few minutes to write an affirmation of their own. When they have finished, invite volunteers to read their affirmations aloud two or three times. Coach them to increase their level of conviction with each repetition. (Try "metering" applause from the class and awarding ratings.) Urge the students to post their affirmations in a prominent location, and remember to repeat them often.

DISCUSSION QUESTIONS

1. Why do we say negative things to ourselves?
2. What's the best way to break a bad habit?
3. What's the best way to form a new habit?
4. How does it feel to say something positive to yourself?
5. Is it easier to say positive things about other people than about yourself? Why?

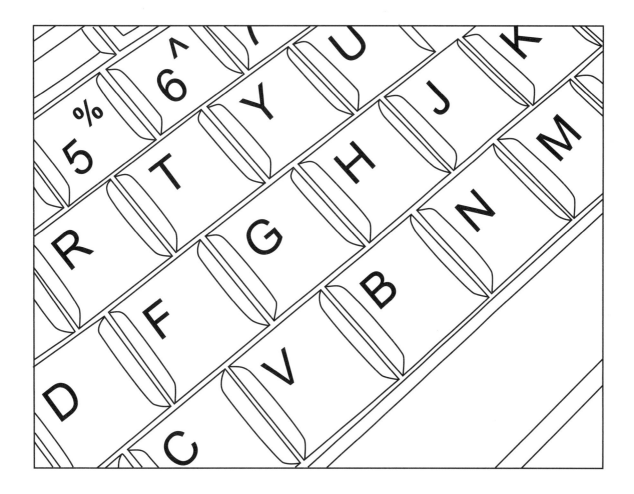

A positive affirmation is like a program that you write for your brain. Positive affirmations help you become the person you want to be. Here are several examples of positive affirmations:

1. I am a good student and enjoy my studies.
2. I love getting good grades and do so easily.
3. I am a good friend, and the other kids like me.
4. I am well organized and get things done on time.
5. I am proud to be on a team and play my best in every game.

Think of something that you want to do better. Write a positive affirmation to program your brain for success. Be sure it is…

- Within your control
- Realistic
- Written in the present tense
- Expresses feeling
- Positive, not negative

_____

_____

Now, put your affirmation to work.

1. Read your affirmation several times a day for at least 21 days.
2. Enjoy reading the affirmation.
3. Feel good about the person you are becoming.

SYNOPSIS ON SELF-TALK

EXPERIENCE SHEET AND DISCUSSION

OBJECTIVES

Students will:
- Define the term *self-talk.*
- Give examples of negative and positive self-talk.
- Discuss methods for improving their own self-talk.

MATERIALS

One copy of the experience sheet "Five Steps to Better Self-Talk" for lower-grade students; one copy of the experience sheet "10 Ways to Improve Self-Talk" for upper-grade students

DIRECTIONS

Ask if anyone can explain the meaning of the term "self-talk." Call on volunteers, and help the students reason that self-talk is *talk we direct at ourselves.* Explain:

Self-talk consists of the things you say <u>about</u> yourself <u>to</u> yourself. It can also refer to judgments you make about yourself when talking to someone else. For example, telling yourself or someone else that you are "lousy at math" is what we call negative self-talk. When you say things about yourself that are negative, you are programming your brain to make you behave in those negative ways. When you say positive things about yourself, you are directing your brain to make you behave in positive ways.

Write the headings "Positive Self-talk" and "Negative Self-talk" on the board. Ask the students to help you brainstorm a list of statements under each heading. Suggest that they recall statements they and their friends commonly make to themselves. List items such as:

Negative	Positive
I'm basically lazy.	I'm good at that.
I can't do puzzles.	I always do well in science.
I hate school.	They like me because I'm funny.
Nobody likes me.	I did the best drawing.

Distribute the experience sheets. Tell the students that you want them to pay attention to their self-talk for the next few days and make a deliberate effort to improve it. Explain that the experience sheet contains tips to help them improve their self-talk. Discuss the tips and suggest specific ways to put them to use.

DISCUSSION QUESTIONS

1. What feelings usually accompany negative thoughts or statements about yourself?
2. What feelings accompany positive thoughts or statements about yourself?
3. How could saying "I'm lousy at spelling" possibly help you in spelling?
4. If it doesn't help to say such things, why do we say them?
5. How can you help a friend improve his/her self-talk? How can your friend help you?

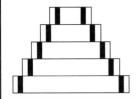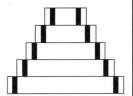

FIVE STEPS TO BETTER SELF-TALK
EXPERIENCE SHEET

1. For the next three days, pay close attention to your self-talk. Keep track of how often you say negative and positive things to yourself.

2. Pay attention to the self-talk of your family and friends.

3. Think of negative self-talk as a bad habit. Replace it with something better.

4. Try to use positive self-talk daily.

5. Tell others how to use positive self-talk.

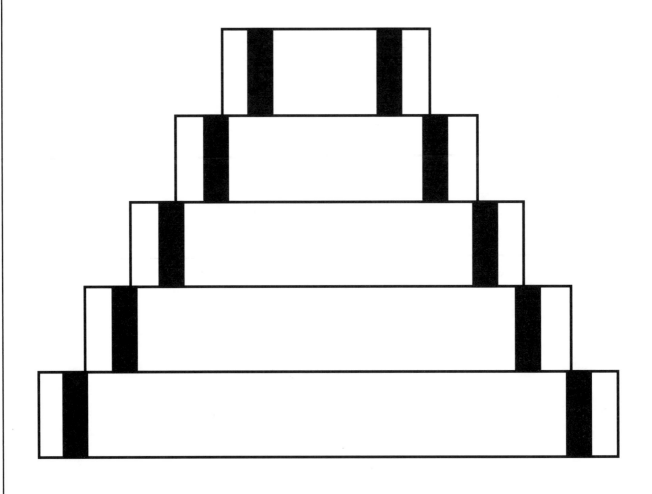

 Less Student Stress, More School Success

10 WAYS TO IMPROVE YOUR SELF-TALK
EXPERIENCE SHEET

1. First, become aware of the problem. For the next three days, pay close attention to your self-talk. Keep track of how frequently you use negative and positive self-talk.

2. Pay attention to the self-talk of other people. How does it influence you?

3. Make a conscious effort to use positive self-talk.

4. A good way to get rid of a bad habit is to replace it with something better.

5. When you catch yourself using negative self-talk, think, "Stop!" Then substitute something positive.

6. When you start to moan and groan about something, think again. Is it really so bad?

7. Statements such as "I can't do this" or "I'll never get this" are especially limiting. First, they are untrue. Second, they stop you from trying.

8. Self-limiting statements increase stress. When something is difficult, thoughts such as "I can't handle this" only make the situation worse. Tell yourself, "I can handle this."

9. Fake it till you make it. When something is tough, tell yourself the challenge is fun. When everything is falling apart, tell yourself, "I'm okay, everything is okay."

10. Encourage others to use positive self-talk.

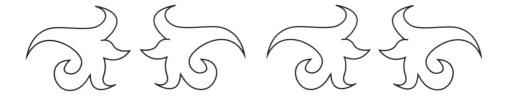

KEEPING TRACK OF TIME

ACTIVITY LOG AND ANALYSIS

OBJECTIVES Students will:
- Complete time logs and analyze the results.
- Evaluate their use of time.
- Identify time-wasters.

MATERIALS Several copies of the experience sheet "My Activity Log" for each student

DIRECTIONS Distribute the experience sheets, basing the number per child on the length of time you plan to have the students log their activities (we recommend three days for lower-grade students and five days for upper-grade students). Explain that the purpose of the activity is to get the students to think about how they spend their time. One of the primary causes of stress is poor time management, which often leaves people rushing to complete some tasks while completely forgetting to do others.

Explain that to manage their time better, the students need to discover how they currently spend their time. Everyone engages in time-wasters that hinder the ability to accomplish goals. Taking a time inventory will help identify time-wasters and enable the students to decide whether to eliminate, reduce, maintain, or increase the time they spend on particular activities.

Have the students write the number of assigned logging days (three or five) on their experience sheets. If possible, have them fill in the dates as well. Suggest that they carry a log sheet with them throughout the day and fill it in as they go. Waiting until the end of the day and then attempting to remember everything does not work well.

Go over the directions for the coding system, which asks the students to code each activity based on its necessity and satisfaction with the amount of time spent. The (+) sign indicates that the activity was both necessary and satisfactory. The (0) sign indicates that the activity was necessary, but unsatisfactory. The (-) sign indicates that the activity was both unnecessary and unsatisfactory.

When the students have finished logging their activities, analyze the results in a follow-up session. Write several activity categories on the board. Choose categories based on the age of your students. Possibilities include socializing, family activities, classwork, homework, phone calls, commuting, shopping, errands, employment, eating, household chores, organized athletics, quiet recreation (TV, computer games, reading, listening to music), and active recreation (tennis, bicycling, dancing). Have the students group their activities in the various categories and add up the amount of time spent in each. Discuss the results.

DISCUSSION QUESTIONS

1. What is your biggest category of activities? What is your smallest?
2. How satisfied are you with the amount of time you spent in each category?
3. What is a time-waster?
4. What are your biggest time-wasters?
5. Do you think time-wasters are contributing to your stress levels? How?
6. Which time-waster would you like to reduce and how will you do it?
7. Why is it important to be aware of how you spend your time?

MY ACTIVITY LOG
EXPERIENCE SHEET

List all of your activities for ___ days. At the end of each day, decide how satisfied you are with the amount of time you spent on each activity. Choose from the codes, below.

+ The activity was <u>necessary</u> and I spent the <u>right amount of time</u>.
- The activity was <u>not necessary</u> and took <u>too much time</u>.
0 The activity was <u>necessary</u> and I spent <u>too much</u> or <u>too little time</u>.

Date: _____

Time	Activity	Satisfaction Level
6:00 a.m.		
6:30 a.m.		
7:00 a.m.		
7:30 a.m.		
8:00 a.m.		
8:30 a.m.		
9:00 a.m.		
9:30 a.m.		
10:00 a.m.		
10:30 a.m.		
11:00 a.m.		
11:30 a.m.		
12:00 noon		
12:30 p.m.		
1:00 p.m.		

©2010 by PRO-ED, Inc. Less Student Stress, More School Success

Time	Activity	Satisfaction Level
1:30 p.m.		
2:00 p.m.		
2:30 p.m.		
3:00 p.m.		
3:30 p.m.		
4:00 p.m.		
4:30 p.m.		
5:00 p.m.		
5:30 p.m.		
6:00 p.m.		
6:30 p.m.		
7:00 p.m.		
7:30 p.m.		
8:00 p.m.		
8:30 p.m.		
9:00 p.m.		
9:30 p.m.		
10:00 p.m.		
10:30 p.m.		
11:00 p.m.		

MANAGING TIME

EXPERIENCE SHEET AND DISCUSSION

OBJECTIVES   Students will:
- Review and discuss time-management skills and techniques.
- Share additional time-management strategies they have tried.

MATERIALS   One copy of the experience sheet "Managing Your Time" for lower-grade students; one copy of the experience sheet "12 Tips for Better Time Management" for upper-grade students

DIRECTIONS   Distribute the experience sheets. Read through the time management tips with the students. Elaborate with examples from your own experience, or the experience of other students you've worked with. Facilitate discussion.

Urge the students to enlist the help of their parents in setting up some of the recommended conditions. Suggest they keep the experience sheets in their notebooks. Occasionally check to see how many have followed the advice provided.

DISCUSSION QUESTIONS
1. Where do you usually study?
2. How well is your study area organized?
3. What tools or supplies do you almost always need for studying?
4. Why do people keep calendars?
5. What would happen if no one wrote down things like medical appointments?
6. Which of the tips on the list do you already use? Which are the most helpful?
7. What are your best study hours?
8. Which of the tips do you think will help you the most?
9. What other ideas do you have for managing time wisely?

Sunday	Monday	Tuesday	Wednesday	Thursday	Friday	Saturday
		1	2	3	4	5
6	7	8	9	10	11	12
13	14	15	16	17	18	19
20	21	22	23	24	25	26
27	28	29	30	31		

Less Student Stress, More School Success

MANAGING YOUR TIME
EXPERIENCE SHEET

1. Get ORGANIZED.
   Keep your room and study area neat and organized. Have things like paper, pencils, eraser, and paper clips nearby. If you use a computer, label files clearly and save them to a "work" folder.

2. Write a daily TO-DO LIST.
   Write down the things you plan to do each day. Cross them off the list when they are done.

3. Learn good STUDY SKILLS.
   Write down assignments. Do the hardest things first. As you read, write down questions to ask the teacher. Outline chapters, or draw diagrams (sometimes called mind-maps).

4. Get enough SLEEP.
   To stay alert and healthy, you need eight or nine hours every night. Your brain is very busy while you sleep. Give it plenty of time to do its work.

5. Don't OVERDO.
   Leave a little time every day for yourself. Time to relax, be with friends, play with your pet, or just do nothing. When you try to do too much, the quality of your work may suffer. Your health may suffer, too.

6. Learn to say NO.
   You don't have to do everything that your friends do. If you are too busy to join them, just say so. Take charge of your time and your choices.

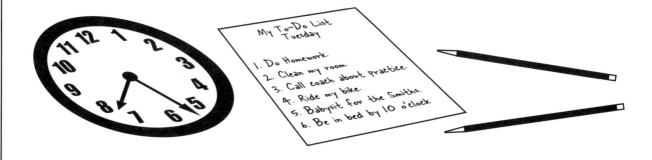

12 TIPS FOR BETTER TIME MANAGEMENT
EXPERIENCE SHEET

1. ORGANIZE your work space.
    You can save a lot of time and grief by keeping your work area tidy. Have things like paper, pencils, eraser, file folders, and paper clips nearby. If you use a computer, keep electronic files organized and clearly labeled.

2. Keep your own CALENDAR.
    Buy an inexpensive wall calendar for your work area. Write down your appointments, activities, and school assignments. Or you may prefer to carry a pocket calendar in your backpack. Choose what works best for you, just be sure to use it.

3. Write a daily TO-DO LIST.
    Write down everything you need to do each day. Then enjoy the good feeling you get from crossing off items as they are completed.

4. PRIORITIZE to-do items.
    A good method is to assign an A, B, or C to each item. Do the A's first, the B's second and the C's third. Don't include appointments, practices, and other scheduled items. Those are commitments that you must keep.

5. PLAN AHEAD.
    When you get an important assignment, look at your calendar and figure out where to schedule the time needed to complete it. Don't wait until the last minute.

6. Learn effective STUDY SKILLS.
    Take good notes. Split big assignments into smaller pieces. Complete the most difficult tasks first. As you read, write down questions to ask the teacher. Outline chapters, or draw diagrams (sometimes called mind-maps).

 Less Student Stress, More School Success

7. Work during your PEAK HOURS.

   Figure out when you do your best work. If you are more alert in the morning, get up extra early to study. If right after school is ideal, try to arrange your schedule to allow an hour or two of study time. Don't give homework the leftovers. Give it your best shot.

8. Review STUDY NOTES daily.

   Every time you go over an idea, formula, or fact, you are building a better memory. When you review daily you won't need to cram before tests.

9. Get enough SLEEP.

   No one functions well on four hours of sleep. You need eight or nine hours every night. Remember, your brain stays very busy while you sleep. It organizes information, makes memories, and repairs and replenishes your body. Give it plenty of time to do its work.

10. Avoid OVERLOAD.

    It's fun to be busy, but don't overdo it. Leave a little time every day for yourself. Time to relax, be with friends, play with your pet, or just do nothing. When you try to do too much, the quality of your performance may suffer. Your health may suffer, too.

11. Learn to say NO.

    Part of avoiding overload is learning to say "no" occasionally. Just explain that your schedule is full and you don't have time. Be firm. Most people will understand.

12. Be FLEXIBLE.

    At times, you may need to rearrange your calendar, or revise your priorities. When something very important comes along, be willing to move things around in order to fit it in.

HIGH-STAKES TESTING

STRATEGIES FOR HANDLING TEST ANXIETY
EXPERIENCE SHEET AND DISCUSSION

OBJECTIVES Students will:
- Describe the physical and psychological effects of test anxiety.
- Compare imagined consequences of failure with realistic consequences.
- Identify stress-reduction techniques that can be used to reduce test anxiety.

MATERIALS One copy of the experience sheet "Easing Test Anxiety" for each student

DIRECTIONS Begin by discussing the concept of test anxiety. Ask the students how much they worry about upcoming tests, the extent to which their lives are disrupted by test anxiety, and how they usually handle it.

At some point in the discussion, ask: "What is the absolute worst thing that could happen if you didn't do well on a test?" Encourage the students to describe the most extreme consequences they can think of. Then ask, "Okay, now that we've imagined the very worst, what do you think would *really* happen?"

Contrast the differences between the students' imaginings and their reality. Point out that the emotions experienced during extreme test anxiety are usually not reality-based. They are better suited to a natural disaster than they are to a test. That is why it's so important to learn and practice stress-reduction skills.

Distribute the experience sheets and go over the directions. Give the students a few minutes to complete the sheets. Then call on volunteers to read items from their lists. Record ideas for reducing test anxiety on the board and discuss ways to implement them prior to and during a test.

DISCUSSION QUESTIONS
1. What can you do if you know an answer, but your mind goes blank?
2. Why is it important to get lots of sleep the night before a test?
3. Why is cramming for a test a bad idea?
4. What messages can you give yourself (self talk) to help reduce test anxiety?
5. What breathing exercises can you use? When should you use them?

EASING TEST ANXIETY
EXPERIENCE SHEET

Tests can be stressful. Even if you study hard, you can still mess up. Lots of worrying about the test only makes the situation worse. But stress can be managed. You have learned several ways to reduce stress and feel more relaxed. Next time you are anxious about a test, try some of those strategies.

DIRECTIONS

In the left-hand column, list ways in which test anxiety affects you (upset stomach, headache, jitters, forgetfulness, etc.). In the right-hand column, list things that you can do reduce the stress.

HOW TEST ANXIETY AFFECTS ME   WHAT I CAN DO TO LOWER THE ANXIETY

1. _____   • _____
   _____   _____

2. _____   • _____
   _____   _____

3. _____   • _____
   _____   _____

4. _____   • _____
   _____   _____

5. _____   • _____
   _____   _____

6. _____   • _____
   _____   _____

7. _____   • _____
   _____   _____

8. _____   • _____
   _____   _____

9. _____   • _____
   _____   _____

10. _____   • _____
    _____   _____

                       Less Student Stress, More School Success

HELPING KIDS WITH TEST ANXIETY
EXPERIENCE SHEET AND DISCUSSION

OBJECTIVES

Students will:
- Describe how test taking affects them emotionally.
- Discuss the importance of reducing the stress of test taking.
- Learn stress-reduction strategies to use in testing situations.

MATERIALS

One copy of the experience sheet "Six Steps to Less Test Stress" for lower-grade students; one copy of the experience sheet "De-stressing the Test" for upper-grade students

DIRECTIONS

Explain to the students that test anxiety is normal and usually not a problem. It's a type of *performance* fear—like feeling nervous before making a speech or playing in a music recital. It can help focus your mind and improve performance.

Extreme anxiety, on the other hand, can be debilitating. Chemicals released by the brain can block memory and result in a lower score. That's why it's important to learn ways to control stress levels, particularly at test time.

Ask the students to recall a recent test situation and describe how they felt just before the test. Write their contributions on the board. Include feelings such as:

- Scared
- Annoyed
- Confident
- Jittery
- Relaxed
- Paralyzed

Distribute the experience sheets and go over the stress-reduction strategies with the students. Elaborate on each one and generate additional suggestions from the group. Suggest that the students keep the sheets in their notebooks as a reminder of things they can do to lessen test stress.

DISCUSSION QUESTIONS

1. Why do teachers and schools give so many tests?
2. What's the best way to make sure you do well on tests?
3. What should you do if you don't understand a test question?
4. Is it okay to guess if you don't know the answer? Why or why not?
5. Which methods of reducing test stress do you already use?
6. What new method do you plan to try?

Having a test? Don't let stress ruin your day – or your score. Take these steps to lower stress.

1. **Prepare.** Read. Do your homework. Ask questions. Enjoy learning. If you do these things, your test scores will be fine.

2. **Get lots of sleep.** Your brain and body need rest. Sleep at least eight hours the night before a test.

3. **Eat breakfast.** Good food makes for a good performance. Skip the sugary stuff. How about some oatmeal and fruit?

4. **Think positive.** Tell yourself that you are going to do exceptionally well on the test. Believe it!

5. **Picture success.** Imagine yourself calmly taking the test and remembering everything you need to know. Have this daydream often.

6. **Ask for help.** If you still get very nervous before tests, talk it over with your teacher or counselor. They can help.

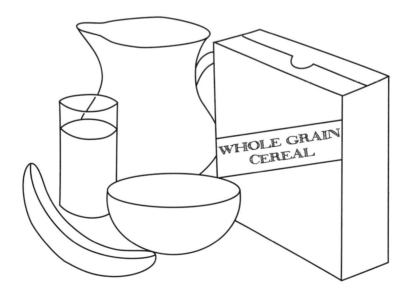

WHOLE GRAIN CEREAL

Less Student Stress, More School Success

DE-STRESSING THE TEST
EXPERIENCE SHEET

It's normal to feel a bit nervous before a test. A little tension can help you stay alert and perform well. But if you are one of those people who panics at the mere thought of a test, you need to find effective ways to de-stress the entire testing experience.

Be prepared. Learn the material. Do the homework. Study and review a little each day. If you keep up with your assignments, you will feel much more confident at test time. Above all, avoid last minute cramming.

Get plenty of rest. The night before the test, get at least eight hours of sleep. Your brain does a lot of important work while you sleep. Give it time.

Eat healthful foods. Fix yourself a nutritious breakfast on the day of the test. If the test is in the afternoon, eat a light lunch. Skip the sugary and salty snacks. Good food aids performance.

Watch your self talk. While preparing for the test, tell yourself that you are ready, relaxed, and confident. Think about what a good memory you have, and how easily you solve most problems. Avoid negative, discouraging thoughts.

Don't expect perfection. Everyone makes mistakes. Very few test takers know all the answers. Do the best you can, but remember that you are human—which means definitely not perfect.

Be on time. Get up early on the day of the test. Give yourself plenty of time to get ready so you don't have to rush. The key is to stay calm and relaxed, which is almost impossible when you are running late.

Take a moment alone. Before the test begins, go somewhere where you can be alone for a few moments. Take some deep breaths and concentrate on relaxing and centering yourself.

Visualize success. Frequently picture yourself calmly and confidently taking tests, easily remembering what you know and answering questions correctly. Be sure to do this just before any test.

Ask for help. If, after trying these strategies, you still find yourself overwhelmed with stress prior to tests, discuss the problem with a counselor, teacher, or other adult. They can help you find ways to get your fear under control.

TEST PREP
RELAXATION AND VISUALIZATION

OBJECTIVES   Students will:
- Practice deep breathing and relaxation techniques.
- Visualize themselves performing well on a test.
- Describe ways of maintaining confidence during actual tests.

MATERIALS   None

DIRECTIONS   Tell the students that you are going to lead them in a short guided visualization that will help them perform well on tests. (If possible, time this activity to precede an actual achievement test, or other significant test.)

Sit in a comfortable position with your hands in your lap and your eyes closed. Take several deep breaths. With each in-breath, feel your body grow warm and calm. With each out-breath, feel your muscles relax.

Gradually let go of any tension. Feel your arms and shoulders relax. Feel your neck and back relax. Let the warmth and relaxation spread to your stomach and hips. Feel it extend to your legs and feet. Continue to focus on your breathing as your entire body relaxes.

Now picture yourself in class. It is test day. You know that it is test day and yet you are completely relaxed. You are confident. You know that you will do your best work. Picture your teacher passing out the test. See the test booklet (paper) in front of you on your desk. Your hands are steady and your mind is calm. You are completely confident and relaxed.

Hear the teacher telling you to start. Picture yourself calmly opening the test booklet and reading the directions. They are clear and you understand them. You feel completely relaxed and ready to begin.

Imagine yourself answering the questions, one at a time. You are alert and relaxed. Your thinking is clear. You can remember what you have learned. Your brain supplies the answers.

As you work through the test, see yourself pausing occasionally to stretch and take a few deep breaths. When you go back to the test, feel yourself refreshed and eager to continue.

Now, think to yourself, "On test day I am relaxed and alert, calm and confident."

When you are ready, open your eyes and come back to the present.

Less Student Stress, More School Success

Give the students a few moments to come back to reality. Then facilitate a follow-up discussion.

DISCUSSION QUESTIONS

1. Why is it important to stay relaxed during tests?
2. What can you do if you feel yourself getting worried or tense during a test?
3. Why do teachers give tests? Why do schools give achievement tests?
4. Why do most people feel nervous before a test?
5. How does it help to picture yourself doing well on a test?

SPELLING TEST 100%

1. *geography*
2. *telephone*
3. *question*
4. *volcano*
5. *feline*
6. *fortunate*
7. *yesterday*
8. *examination*
9. *poetry*
10. *knickers*

ANGER AND WORRY

UNDERSTANDING ANGER
EXPERIENCE SHEET AND DISCUSSION

OBJECTIVES   Students will:
- Identify situations, people, and conditions that trigger anger.
- Describe emotional and cognitive responses that often lead to anger.

MATERIALS   One copy of the experience sheet "What Makes Me Angry" for each student

DIRECTIONS   Initiate a discussion about anger and things that trigger it. Point out that no one gets angry without a reason. It may not always be a good reason, but something triggers the anger—a word, a gesture, a dangerous or unfair situation, or having to do something we don't want to do. Tell the students that you are going to give them a few minutes to list things that tend to make them angry.

Distribute the experience sheets and give the students time to complete them. Then ask volunteers to share some of the items they listed. Write key words on the board under the heading "Anger Triggers." If two or more students name the same trigger, keep track of the number by adding check marks after the item.

When you have generated a number of triggers, question the students about their feelings leading up to the anger. Look for common underlying feelings. For example:
- You fail an exam and think your parents will be angry. (fear)
- You share a secret with a friend, who spreads it around. (embarrassment)
- You disagree with someone about an important matter. (desire to win or be "right")
- You are placed on restriction until you clean your room. (frustration)
- You lose an important game. (disappointment, strong desire to win)
- Your teacher corrects or criticizes you in front of classmates. (embarrassment)
- Someone threatens to hit you. (fear)
- Someone does hit you. (pain, frustration)
- Your parents refuse to let you go somewhere with friends. (disappointment, frustration)
- Your friends ignore you, or leave you out of an activity. (embarrassment, humiliation)

Point out that anger is often either defensive or retaliatory. We use anger to protect ourselves from physical or emotional injury. Or we use anger to get back at people who hurt us in some way. Sometimes we start "protecting" ourselves before anything even happens, such as when we feel angry every time we see a person we don't like, or face a test in a subject in which we do poorly.

Urge the students to try to become aware of what's really happening when they start to get angry. By doing so, they will become more self-aware and better able to control their anger.

DISCUSSION QUESTIONS

1. What does getting angry accomplish?
2. In what other ways, besides getting angry, could you express frustration? Embarrassment? Fear?
3. How does your body feel when you are starting to get angry?
4. What other clues tell you that you are starting to get angry?
5. What can you do to stop an angry response when you first sense it?

Less Student Stress, More School Success

WHAT MAKES ME ANGRY
EXPERIENCE SHEET

Think back over the last few days or weeks. When did you feel angry? Try to remember what caused your anger in each situation. List all the causes you can think of below.

1. _____

_____

2. _____

_____

3. _____

_____

4. _____

_____

5. _____

_____

6. _____

_____

7. _____

_____

8. _____

_____

9. _____

_____

10. _____

_____

CAUSES OF ANGER

EXPERIENCE SHEET AND DISCUSSION

OBJECTIVES   Students will:
- Identify people, conditions, and situations that tend to make them angry.
- Describe constructive ways to manage their anger.

MATERIALS   One copy of the experience sheet "What Sets Me Off" for each student

DIRECTIONS   Engage the students in a discussion about anger. Acknowledge that it is an uncomfortable emotion that can sometimes be difficult to control. However, emphasize that it is normal to feel angry at times, and that anger can play a useful role in day-to-day life. Make these additional points:
- Anger is a normal human emotion. It is neither bad nor good.
- Sometimes anger serves a protective function.
- Volatile expressions of anger, if they happen often, can have negative health consequences.
- There are healthy and appropriate ways to manage anger.
- It is how we react to a situation, not the situation itself, that causes anger and other emotions.

Distribute the experience sheets and go over the directions. Give the students a few minutes to list situations and conditions that make them angry and ways to manage the anger. When they have finished, ask volunteers to read some of their items to the group. Elaborate on each example and use it to generate further discussion. Focus less on the situations (and their justification) and more on anger-management strategies.

DISCUSSION QUESTIONS
1. Why is it important to control anger?
2. What are the most common causes of anger in our group?
3. What ideas for controlling anger work best for you?
4. What new ideas for controlling anger would you like to try?
5. What can you do if nothing you try helps to lessen your anger?

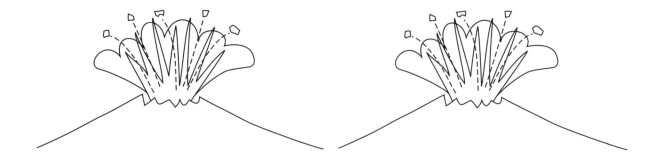

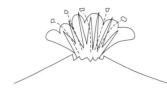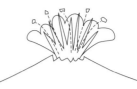

WHAT SETS ME OFF
EXPERIENCE SHEET

Do certain things almost always make you angry? Do you react angrily to the same situations—or the same people—over and over? Maybe you get angry when you don't get your way. Or when your brother or sister uses your things without asking.

In the left column, list things that usually make you angry. In the right column, list things you can do to deal with your angry feelings.

What Makes Me Angry	What I Can Do
1. _____	_____
2. _____	_____
3. _____	_____
4. _____	_____
5. _____	_____
6. _____	_____
7. _____	_____
8. _____	_____
9. _____	_____
10. _____	_____

EXPRESSING ANGER CONSTRUCTIVELY
ANGER TRACKING AND DISCUSSION

OBJECTIVES   Students will:
- Describe ways in which people respond when angry.
- Differentiate constructive responses from destructive responses.
- Learn how to formulate an I-message.
- Monitor and record their own anger responses over several days.

MATERIALS   Several copies of the experience sheet "Anger Response Record" for each student

DIRECTIONS   Briefly review earlier lessons and concepts related to anger and anger management. Then ask the students to describe how they and others often respond when angry. Ask, "What have you seen people do or say when they are angry? What do you usually do yourself?"

List behaviors on the board, such as:
- Yell, shout
- Argue, fight
- Clam up, refuse to communicate
- Walk away
- Hit, strike, spank
- Cry
- Throw things
- Kick or punch objects
- Take a time out
- Count to 10

Go back over the list and ask the students which behaviors could be considered constructive, and which are generally destructive. For example, walking away can be constructive if doing so gives people a chance to calm down. Kicking and punching is destructive if people are hurt or property is damaged, but punching a pillow or kicking a ball is constructive if it helps relieve the anger. Facilitate discussion and debate. Older students are likely to disagree about the utility of responses like arguing and "fair" fighting. Rather than impose a particular set of values, encourage critical thinking.

As an alternative to yelling, name-calling, and blaming, teach the students how to confront the other person with an I-message. Add "I-message" to the list on the board and explain that an I-message is a statement that describes how the other person's behavior (or the situation) affects you and how you feel as a result. Show the students the difference between a blaming message and an I-message by giving a few examples, such as:

"You're a liar. You never keep your promises." vs. "When you don't keep a promise, I feel like I can't trust you."

"It's not your turn, so stop crowding in, you bully!" vs. "I was next, and I think you should wait your turn."

Set aside time in a future session to have the students practice formulating I-messages.

Distribute the experience sheets and briefly review the questions. You might want to give each student one sheet initially. Once you have buy-in, encourage the students to take several sheets so that they can monitor their anger for a full week.

At the end of the monitoring period, invite the students to share some of their experiences (without using names) and describe their responses. Facilitate discussion.

DISCUSSION QUESTIONS

1. How did filling out the sheets affect your responses to anger?
2. What did you learn about the way you respond to anger?
3. If you tried using an I-message, how did it go?
4. What response worked best for you? Was it constructive or destructive?
5. What responses made things worse?
6. How has your ability to manage anger improved as a result of this activity?

 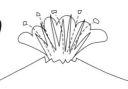

ANGER RESPONSE RECORD
EXPERIENCE SHEET

Track your anger for one week. Take a few minutes to complete a sheet like this when:

- You are *starting* to feel angry about something or someone.
- You *already* got angry about something or someone.

1. Describe the situation and who is (or was) involved. _____

_____

2. How angry are (or were) you? Circle one.
   - Annoyed
   - Cross
   - Steamed
   - Mad
   - Furious
   - Enraged
   - Out of control

3. How will (or did) you respond? _____

_____

4. What other choices do (or did) you have? _____

_____

5. What will (or did) your response accomplish? _____

_____

6. How will (or did) the situation end? _____

_____

 Less Student Stress, More School Success

FACE TO FACE

ROLE-PLAYING AND DISCUSSION

OBJECTIVES   Students will:
- Role-play a conflict situation, playing both parts.
- Communicate the point of view of a person with whom they disagree or are angry.
- Explain how understanding the opposition's point of view can help relieve anger and resolve conflict.

MATERIALS   This activity requires two moveable chairs for each participating student. After you read the directions, decide whether you want all of the students to participate at once, a few at a time, or one at a time. Counselors working with mature students may prefer to work with one student at a time, with the other students observing and participating in a debriefing session following each imagined confrontation.

DIRECTIONS   Tell the students that they are going to participate in an exercise that will help them to understand the point of view of someone with whom they are angry or have a disagreement. Explain that most people, when angry, see only one point of view— their own. But with a little imagination, it's possible to understand other points of view, which can go a long way toward resolving differences.

Place pairs of chairs facing each other. Give the following directions to participating students:

1. Sit in one chair and face the other (empty) chair.
2. Imagine the person you are angry with seated opposite you, in the empty chair.
3. Tell the person in the empty chair the things he or she has done that upset you. Use I-messages or any other form of communication that effectively expresses your feelings.
4. Now, switch chairs and imagine that you are the person with whom you are angry. For example, if you are angry at a friend, become the friend and speak from his or her point of view in response to what you just said.
5. Switch chairs and become yourself again. Respond from your own point of view.

Circulate and coach the students as they continue their individual confrontations, playing both roles and switching chairs as they represent alternate, or opposing, points of view.

Focus a follow-up discussion on the importance of trying to understand the views of others, particularly in conflict situations.

DISCUSSION QUESTIONS

1. Why is it important to understand the point of view of someone with whom you are angry or disagree?
2. What's the difference between understanding the other person's viewpoint and "giving in" to the other person?
3. What role does listening play in understanding the views of others?
4. What did you learn from playing the role of your "opponent" in this exercise?
5. What did your "opponent" learn about you?
6. What would happen if you had this conversation in real life? Would it help settle the problem?

For younger children:

Have the students imagine a worry or anxiety sitting in the empty chair; for example, fear of the dark, or of spiders. Encourage them to imagine the worry or anxiety having the form and features of a friendly monster. Then instruct the students to have a conversation with the monster, switching chairs and playing both roles. Encourage the students to ask the monster questions that will help them understand the worry. Follow the activity with a discussion.

Less Student Stress, More School Success

THE POWER OF ANGER
EXPERIENCE SHEET AND DISCUSSION

OBJECTIVES Students will:
- Identify feelings and sensations associated with anger.
- Graphically describe how anger makes them feel.
- Discuss the importance of controlling anger.

MATERIALS One copy of the experience sheet "How Anger Feels" for each student

DIRECTIONS Begin by facilitating a discussion about the feelings and sensations generated by anger. For example, ask:
- How does your body feel when you are angry?
- What happens to your energy level when you are angry?
- How well are you able to study?
- What affect does being angry have on sleep?

Distribute the experience sheets. Review the list of responses on the first page. Ask for a show of hands from students who have experienced each one as a result of being angry. Invite volunteers to elaborate, describe specific situations (no names), and suggest other feelings and sensations generated by anger.

Go over the directions for the second page of the experience sheets, and give the students a few minutes to complete it. Conduct a debriefing session. Ask volunteers to share their drawings and describe the feelings and sensations represented. Discuss what the students have observed about anger and what it does to their bodies and minds.

Conclude by reminding students that they have the power to control anger.

DISCUSSION QUESTIONS
1. What kinds of things make you angry?
2. What do you usually do when you are angry?
3. What helps you get over being angry?
4. How does it feel to be around someone who is very angry?
5. Why should people avoid making decisions when they are angry?

HOW ANGER FEELS
EXPERIENCE SHEET

Think about times you have been angry. Put a (✔) mark in front of any item that describes you when you are angry.

____ My stomach churns.
____ My head hurts.
____ I clench my teeth.
____ My face turns hot and red.
____ My heart races.
____ My body trembles.
____ My brain gets jumbled and I can't think clearly.
____ I feel like screaming.
____ I feel like crying.
____ My facial features scowl, frown, or grimace.
____ I want to hit something with my fists.

List other feelings here:

- _____
- _____
- _____

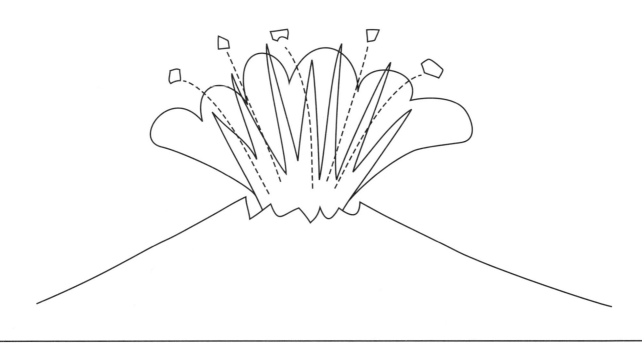

 Less Student Stress, More School Success

DIRECTIONS

Using the outline below, draw a picture of yourself when you are angry. Draw your angry features. Use colors and symbols to show how your body feels when you are angry.

Anger is normal. Everyone feels angry sometimes. But anger is a powerful emotion. It can make you feel terrible. And it can make you say and do things that you later regret.

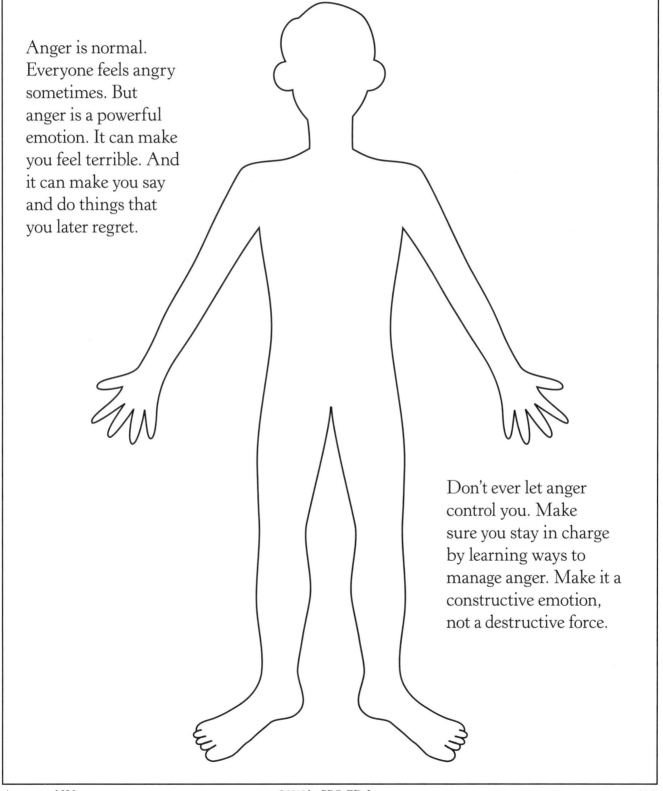

Don't ever let anger control you. Make sure you stay in charge by learning ways to manage anger. Make it a constructive emotion, not a destructive force.

TAMING TEMPERS

EXPERIENCE SHEET AND DISCUSSION

OBJECTIVES   Students will:
- Brainstorm ways of defusing negative energy before it erupts in anger.
- Commit to testing specific anger-management strategies.

MATERIALS   One copy of the experience sheet "Tips for Taming Your Temper" for each student

DIRECTIONS   Ask the students to think of ways they can appropriately express the energy that builds up inside as a result of anger. Write their suggestions on the board and discuss.

Divide the class into groups of three or four. Have the groups brainstorm additional acceptable ways of dealing with anger. Ask each group to share two or three ideas with the class.

Remind the students that if they know what makes them angry, they can learn to recognize the onset of angry feelings and can do something to calm down or cool down.

Distribute the experience sheets and read through the temper-taming tips together. Give the students a few minutes to complete the sheet by listing five ideas they are willing to try the next few times they feel themselves getting angry.

DISCUSSION QUESTIONS
1. Why is it important to learn techniques for managing anger?
2. What happens when people are unable to control their anger?
3. What techniques for reducing anger have worked for you?
4. Why is physical exercise so effective at reducing anger?
5. What happens if you let anger build up inside over hours or days?

TIPS FOR TAMING YOUR TEMPER
EXPERIENCE SHEET

- Ride a bike.
- Go for a jog.
- Fast dance to loud music.
- Skateboard.
- Scream into a pillow.
- Hit a stuffed toy.
- Jump rope.
- Swim.
- Skate.
- Punch a pillow or punching bag.
- Cry.
- Write a letter and tear it up.
- Talk it over with a good listener.
- Talk to someone you trust.
- Use conflict management strategies.
- Count to 10 or higher.

- Talk to yourself in a positive way.
- Tense and relax your muscles.
- Squeeze a ball.
- Read a book.
- Listen to music.
- Run in place for three minutes.
- Take 10 deep breaths.
- Write your feelings in a journal.
- Take a one-minute daydream vacation to your favorite place.
- Play with a pet.
- Draw or paint a picture.
- Play a sport.
- Play a musical instrument.
- Take a hot shower or bath.

List five ideas that you can use to tame your temper when you are angry. Choose from the above list, or write down ideas of your own.

1. _____

2. _____

3. _____

4. _____

5. _____

WORRIES AND SOLUTIONS

TEAM COMPETITION

OBJECTIVES   Students will:
- Identify worries commonly experienced by students.
- Suggest solutions to common worries.

MATERIALS   None

DIRECTIONS   Begin by having the students brainstorm things that kids their age frequently worry about. Write the worries on the board. Encourage the students to name things related to friends, social standing, school, grades, parents, siblings, physical appearance, health, schedules, athletics, chores, organizations, and activities.

Spend a few minutes talking about the amount of time spent worrying about things that:

1. could be resolved by putting the same energy into developing solutions, or
2. never actually happen.

Divide the class evenly into two teams. Designate one the "Worrywarts" and the other the "Resolvers." Have the members of the two teams gather on opposite sides of the room. Ask one Worrywart and one Resolver to come to the center (or front) of the room and face each other.

Direct the Worrywart to choose one worry from the list on the board and start worrying about it—aloud. Encourage the Worrywart to choose a worry that he or she can relate to, and then to dramatize it fully, stating all the reasons why it is such a big concern.

Direct the Resolver to offer suggestions about how to avoid the problem, solve the problem, or deal calmly with the worry in order to lessen the stress. Encourage the Resolver to be creative, confident, and persistent.

Direct the rest of the students to listen for workable solutions and suggestions.

Signal the two sides to begin the exchange. Coach them to play their roles enthusiastically, but don't allow them to talk over each other to the extent that no one can hear what is being said.

After a few minutes, stop the action and debrief the players and the class. Ask the Worrywarts (especially the player) if they heard any solutions or advice that could relieve the worry. If so, award a point to the Resolvers.

Continue the contest with a new pair of players and a new worry. About halfway through the allotted time, have the teams switch roles and names, so that both sides have an opportunity to offer solutions and win points.

DISCUSSION QUESTIONS

1. How difficult was it to think of realistic solutions?
2. Was it easier to be a Worrywart, or a Resolver? Why?
3. What can you do about a worry that involves other people?
4. When was the last time you worried about something needlessly?
5. When is worry a useful emotion? When is it a waste of time? When is it destructive?

EXERCISE

LIFETIME FITNESS

EXPERIENCE SHEET AND DISCUSSION

OBJECTIVES   Students will:
- Define four types of fitness and describe exercises that build each type.
- Explain how frequency, intensity, and time affect exercise benefits.
- Describe the benefits of regular exercise.

MATERIALS   One copy of the experience sheet "Exercise and Fitness" for each student

DIRECTIONS   Distribute the experience sheets. On the board, write the headings, "Cardiovascular," "Muscle Strength," "Endurance," and "Flexibility." Ask a volunteer to read the definition of each type of fitness from the experience sheet. Brainstorm exercises that fit in each category and write them on the board while the students list them on their sheets.

Explain that three components are necessary to establish a fitness program. Suggest that the students use the acronym **FIT** as an easy way to remember *how often* (F=frequency), *how hard* (I=intensity), and for *how long* (T-time) to exercise.

Discuss the following information with the students:

Frequency: Simply to maintain a good fitness level requires three sessions of aerobic activity a week. If a person wants to improve his or her level of fitness, more time is required.

Intensity: Intensity is measured in heartbeats per minute and is monitored during exercise by checking pulse rate. Every person has a working heart-rate range, which is calculated based on resting heart rate and age. Within that range, higher heart rates during exercise build cardiovascular fitness; lower heart rates are best for burning fat.

Time: To obtain maximum benefits from physical activity, heart rate must be maintained within an individual's working range nonstop for 20 to 30 minutes. To lose weight, people need to exercise a minimum of one hour.

Warming up and cooling down for several minutes before and after exercise further maximizes benefits and helps guard against injuries.

Finally, brainstorm and discuss the benefits of regular exercise. Include:

- Stress reduction
- More energy
- Better health
- Longer life
- Improved self-image
- More attractive appearance
- Weight management
- Higher academic achievement
- Improved social life

DISCUSSION QUESTIONS

1. Given all these benefits, why would anyone *not* want to exercise?
2. What's the best way to develop the *habit* of exercising?
3. What forms of exercise have you tried, but not pursued?
4. How can you avoid getting discouraged if you don't do well the first time you try something?
5. How does general fitness level affect enjoyment of an activity like running?

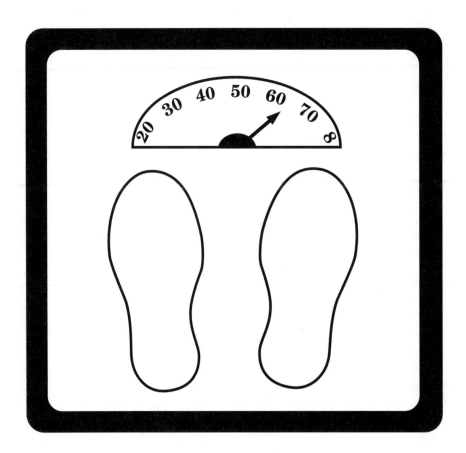

EXERCISE AND FITNESS
EXPERIENCE SHEET

Cardiovascular Fitness: The ability of the heart and lungs to take in and use oxygen. Aerobic exercises increase and maintain cardiovascular fitness. Examples of aerobic exercise are:

1. _____
2. _____
3. _____
4. _____
5. _____

Muscle Strength: The ability of muscles to apply or exert force. Strength-training exercises are often different from aerobic exercises. Examples of strength training exercises are:

1. _____
2. _____
3. _____

Endurance: The ability of muscles to continue an activity over an extended period of time without tiring. Good endurance allows a person to exercise longer. Endurance is important in activities such as:

1. _____
2. _____
3. _____

Flexibility: The ability to move muscles and joints to their full extent, without strain. Flexible muscles are the best guard against muscle pulls, strains, and other injuries. Regular stretching increases flexibility. Activities that require lots of flexibility include:

1. _____
2. _____
3. _____

ACTION PLANNING

EXPERIENCE SHEET AND DISCUSSION

OBJECTIVES   Students will:
- Write a fitness goal and develop an action plan for achieving it.
- Identify potential roadblocks to achieving their goals and devise ways around them.
- Understand that a goal is a commitment, or a promise, made to themselves.

MATERIALS   One copy of the experience sheet "Fitness Goal and Plan" for each student

DIRECTIONS   Distribute the experience sheets. Instruct each student to develop one specific fitness goal. Write some examples on the board. Point out what makes them specific.

- To walk two miles, three times a week.
- To jog three miles every other morning on the school track.
- To enroll in a gymnastics class that meets two afternoons a week.

Tell the students to think of things that might keep them from reaching their goals. Suggest that they include all of the excuses they typically give themselves for not exercising, such as not having enough time, being too tired, feeling embarrassed, or not having a friend to exercise with. After they have listed their roadblocks, emphasize that the students must be prepared to overcome these roadblocks if they hope to reach their goals.

Working in pairs, have the students brainstorm ways to overcome each other's roadblocks. Solutions might include scheduling exercise on the family calendar, going to bed earlier, and asking a friend to join them.

Point out that once the roadblocks are removed, the goal can be reached more easily, but *not* automatically. A plan must be developed with specific steps that lead the student toward the goal. Emphasize that effective action planning includes every small step that must be taken. It might also include helpful assists, such as laying out exercise clothes the night before.

Give some examples of positive self-talk, or affirmations, that will help motivate the students to pursue their goals. For example:

"Jogging gives me energy."
"I feel good after I exercise."
"My fitness is improving every day."

Suggest that the students pledge to reward themselves if they succeed in sticking with their plans for one month. Urge them to choose obtainable rewards that will further encourage their fitness efforts. Finally, stress that their goals are promises that they have made to themselves. Urge them to honor their commitments.

DISCUSSION QUESTIONS

1. Is your fitness goal completely new, or is it one you've attempted before? If you've attempted it before, what happened?
2. What excuses do you typically use to avoid exercise?
3. Which of your roadblocks are just excuses, and which are real concerns?
4. If something interferes with your exercise schedule, how will you make up the time?
5. What are some of the steps you must take to reach your goal?
6. How do you plan to reward yourself?

MY FITNESS GOAL AND PLAN
EXPERIENCE SHEET

When you set a goal, you need to think of all the things that might keep you from achieving it. Think of those things as roadblocks. If one crops up, you'll have to remove it (or get around it) in order to reach your goal. Once you solve the problem of roadblocks, you can write down the specific steps you will take to reach your goal.

My fitness goal is: _____

Possible roadblocks are: _____

_____

Ways to remove roadblocks:

1. _____

2. _____

3. _____

4. _____

Steps to achieving my goal:

1. _____

2. _____

3. _____

4. _____

5. _____

Use positive self-talk to encourage yourself to stick with the plan. When you reach your goal, or are well on your way to reaching it, reward yourself.

- Positive self-talk statements to encourage myself: _____

_____

- My reward for achieving my fitness goal for one month: _____

_____

          Less Student Stress, More School Success

RATING PHYSICAL FITNESS
EXPERIENCE SHEET AND DISCUSSION

OBJECTIVES   Students will:
- Assess their levels of physical fitness and regular activity.
- Identify obstacles to daily exercise.
- Use a problem-solving process to eliminate obstacles in sample situations.

MATERIALS   One copy of the experience sheet "Getting Physical" for each student

DIRECTIONS   Distribute the experience sheets and give the students a few minutes to answer the questions.

Ask volunteers to share their answers to the first two questions on the inventory. Draw parallels between activities they enjoyed as small children and those they enjoy now. Ask the students to describe the benefits of their current physical activities. Include social, leadership, and self-esteem benefits as well as physical and health benefits.

Point out that the U.S. Surgeon General has stated that children and teens should engage in at least one hour of vigorous physical activity daily. Ask for a show of hands from students who are able to achieve this standard.

Ask the other students to name things that prevent them from getting enough exercise. Is it lack of interest? Lack of time? Lack of equipment? Lack of parental cooperation? Lack of friends to exercise with? Lack of opportunities? Write their answers on the board under the heading "Obstacles."

Take a few minutes to examine one or two of the obstacles in more detail. Once you have clearly defined each problem, brainstorm possible solutions and write them on the board. Encourage the students to be creative in their approach to solving the problems. Urge all of the students to proactively seek solutions to problems that interfere with their getting adequate exercise.

DISCUSSION QUESTIONS
1. What physical activities do your parents pursue?
2. What activities do you do as a family?
3. Why is it helpful to vary your exercise routine?
4. What are some physical activities that don't require equipment?
5. Do kids play spontaneous pickup games in your school or neighborhood? How would you go about joining one?

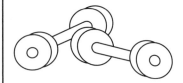

GETTING PHYSICAL
EXPERIENCE SHEET

To some kids, physical education is the best thing about school. They love to be outside—moving, playing, competing, winning, even losing. It's all fun. Other kids dread physical education. To them, it's the worst thing about school, and they will do almost anything to avoid it. What about you?

1. What physical activities did you enjoy when you were a little kid? _____
_____

2. What is your favorite sport or physical activity now? _____
_____

3. Which sports or physical activities do you dislike? Why? _____
_____
_____

4. How much time do you spend exercising each day? _____
_____

5. If you exercise less than one hour a day, what prevents you from doing more? __
_____

6. On a scale of 1 to 10, with 10 being "highly fit," how do you rate your physical fitness? _____
_____

7. What is one thing you can do to improve your physical fitness? _____
_____

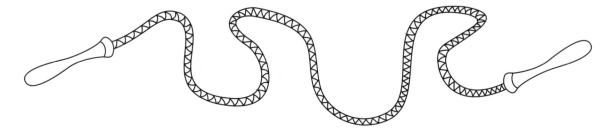

 Less Student Stress, More School Success

ASSESSING HEALTH HABITS
HEALTH INVENTORY AND DISCUSSION

OBJECTIVES

Students will:
- Define "good health."
- Name good health habits and describe their benefits.
- Assess their own health-related behaviors.

MATERIALS

One copy of the experience sheet "Health Inventory" for each student

DIRECTIONS

Begin by discussing the meaning of "good health." Emphasize that good health is much more than the absence of sickness and disease. On a scale of -10 to +10, ask the students to think of being "well" (not sick) as zero, or neutral. There are many things people can do to improve their health and move up the scale, just as there are things people can do to worsen their health and move down the scale.

Ask the students to name behaviors that produce good health when they are practiced routinely. List them on the board under the heading "Good Health Habits." Include items related to diet, exercise, weight management, safety, medical care, cleanliness, sleep, stress, and attitude.

Distribute the experience sheets and go over the directions. Give the students a few minutes to complete the sheet. Ask volunteers to name the areas in which they would like to improve. Question two or three of the volunteers about exactly what they want to achieve (e.g., lose 10 pounds, eat less junk food, jog regularly) and write corresponding goal statements on the board. Urge the students to develop plans for reaching their goals.

Finally, have the students name some of the benefits of having good health habits. Include these benefits on the list:

- More energy
- Improved concentration
- Toned, flexible muscles
- More attractive appearance
- Better complexion
- Fewer colds
- Better grades
- Feeling good

DISCUSSION QUESTIONS

1. How do healthy habits reduce stress?
2. What is your favorite form of exercise?
3. How does exercise help maintain healthy weight?
4. What is your strongest health habit? How did you become strong in that area?
5. How could you change your school routine to make it healthier? What about your home routine?

HEALTH INVENTORY
EXPERIENCE SHEET

Circle one number for each statement. Circle **5** if the item *describes you perfectly*, **4** if it is *mostly true*, **3** if it is *somewhat true*, **2** if it is *mostly untrue*, and **1** if it is *completely untrue*.

1. I eat at least five servings of fruits and vegetables each day. **1 2 3 4 5**

2. My weight is about right for me. **1 2 3 4 5**

3. I get at least one hour of vigorous exercise on most days. **1 2 3 4 5**

4. I have lots of energy. **1 2 3 4 5**

5. I sleep eight or more hours most nights. **1 2 3 4 5**

6. I have regular physical checkups. **1 2 3 4 5**

7. I take my time eating and enjoy meals. **1 2 3 4 5**

8. I rarely eat in fast-food restaurants. **1 2 3 4 5**

9. I believe good health is important. **1 2 3 4 5**

10. I am rarely sick. **1 2 3 4 5**

11. I am in better health than most kids my age. **1 2 3 4 5**

12. I wear my seatbelt when traveling in a vehicle. **1 2 3 4 5**

13. I obey safety rules and laws. **1 2 3 4 5**

14. I prefer water and juice over soft drinks and soda. **1 2 3 4 5**

15. I'd rather eat an apple than a bag of chips. **1 2 3 4 5**

16. When using a computer, I take a break every 20 minutes. **1 2 3 4 5**

17. I visit the dentist at least twice a year. **1 2 3 4 5**

18. There is someone I can talk to when I feel stressed out. **1 2 3 4 5**

19. I usually prefer doing something active to watching TV. **1 2 3 4 5**

20. I manage my time well. **1 2 3 4 5**

Go back and review your ratings. Where can you improve? Put a check mark (✔) next to two items that you are willing to work on. Make those your health goals. If you need help writing a goal statement for each one, ask your teacher, counselor, or parent.

     Less Student Stress, More School Success

A HEALTHY HEART

EXPERIENCE SHEET AND DISCUSSION

OBJECTIVES   Students will:
- Measure their heart rates while resting and after different forms of exercise.
- Explain how exercise contributes to a healthy heart.
- Identify regular forms of exercise in which they participate.

MATERIALS   One copy of the experience sheet "Measuring My Fitness" for each student; crayons or markers

DIRECTIONS   Distribute the experience sheets.

Ask the students to place the palm of one hand over their heart. Ask volunteers to describe what they feel. Explain that the heart is a muscle that they can depend on to pulse, or beat, every few seconds throughout their entire life. Whether they are awake or asleep, it will never stop.

Ask the students why their hearts are beating. Talk about the heart's job of pumping blood throughout the body, and the blood's role in carrying oxygen, nutrients, and other vital substances to the cells. Explain that when they exercise, the body needs more oxygen and nutrients, so the heart pumps faster.

To complete the first part of the experience sheet, have the students begin by measuring their resting heart rate. Tell them to close their eyes, take a few deep breaths and sit very quietly for a few minutes. When they seem relaxed and calm, instruct them to lightly press the first two fingers of right hand against their neck, just below their earlobe (the carotid artery), or against the inside of their left wrist, below the thumb. Demonstrate both positions. Wait until everyone finds a pulse. Then signal the students to start counting. Tell them to stop at exactly one minute, and record the number of beats on their experience sheet. (Or do a six-second count multiplied by 10; a 15-second count multiplied by four; or a 30-second count multiplied by two.)

Take the students outdoors for the rest of the measurements. Have them walk a prescribed course (such as around a basketball court) for two minutes, and then stand still and measure and record their heart rates. Next, have them jog the same course for one or two minutes, again measuring and recording. Finally, have them jump around in place for a minute or two. (You may prefer to substitute calisthenics or dancing for jumping.)

Return to the classroom. Distribute crayons or markers and have the students complete the second part of the experience sheet. When they have finished, have the students hold up their completed exercise grids, showing the boxes filled in with color. Facilitate discussion.

DISCUSSION QUESTIONS

1. What was the difference between your resting heart rate and your fastest heart rate?
2. Could you feel your heart working during strenuous exercise? How did it feel?
3. What happens to muscles (including the heart muscle) when they are exercised regularly?
4. Why is it important to build a strong heart?
5. How many grid squares were you able to fill in with color?
6. How many people filled in squares on every line?
7. Why is it good to get different kinds of exercise?

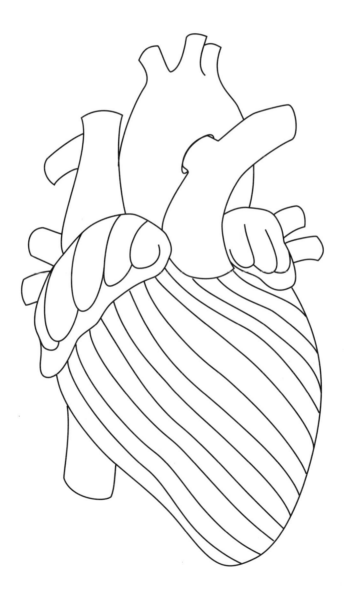

MEASURING MY FITNESS
EXPERIENCE SHEET

What happens to your heart when you exercise? Count the beats per minute and write them on the chart.

ACTIVITY	BEATS PER MINUTE
Sitting quietly	
Fast walking	
Jogging	
Jumping	

Complete the exercise grid. Color the boxes to show what activities you do each day. Use different colors to make a grid pattern.

ACTIVITY	MONDAY	TUESDAY	WEDNESDAY	THURSDAY	FRIDAY
Skip rope					
Ride bike					
Soccer/football					
Softball/Little League					
Skate/skate board					
Jog/run					
Play on playground					
Gymnastics/dance					
Swim					

EXERCISE AND PULSE RATE
EXPERIENCE SHEET AND DISCUSSION

OBJECTIVES   Students will:
- Measure their pulse rates at rest and several times during exercise.
- Compare these measurements to their approximate working heart-rate range.
- Identify activities that promote working-range exercise.

MATERIALS   One copy of the experience sheet "Hitting the Target Range" for each student

DIRECTIONS   Distribute the experience sheets.

Using a timer, have the students measure their pulse rates while seated quietly at their desks. Give them a moment to find their pulse. Then instruct them to count the beats for six seconds. Tell them to multiply the count by 10 to get the total number of beats per minute. This is the resting heart rate. Have the students record this rate on the experience sheet. (Tell the students that the most accurate resting rate is measured upon first waking in the morning, before getting out of bed. Some of the students may want to try this on their own.)

Next, discuss the concept of the "working range." Explain that most people's maximum heart rate (measured in beats per minute, or BPM) is 220 *minus* their age. So, a 16-year old can safely exercise up to 204 BPM. However, the working range is lower. To be within their working range, the students must work hard enough to strengthen their hearts, but not so hard that they can't maintain a vigorous pace for 20 to 30 minutes. An average (and safe) working range for young people is 100 to 170 BPM. Write these numbers on the board and have the students record this range on their experience sheets.

Now, have the students stand and run in place for one minute. Immediately time the students for six seconds while they measure their pulse rates again. Direct them to multiply the number of beats by 10 and record.

Have the students continue to run in place for a total of 10 minutes. Every two minutes, stop the students and take another six-second heart rate. Multiply and record.

Following the final exercise period, have the students rest or stretch for up to five minutes. Then do another six-second count, multiply and record. Explain that this is the students' recovery heart rate. It indicates how quickly the heart "recovers" from exercise. In general, the faster the recovery, the fitter the heart.

Less Student Stress, More School Success

Have the students complete the remainder of the experience sheet. Conclude the activity with a discussion.

DISCUSSION QUESTIONS

1. How did your heart rate change throughout the 10 minutes of exercise?
2. How do you remember feeling when your heart rate was at its highest?
3. What effect does exercise have on a healthy heart?
4. If you exceeded your working range during the workout, what does that tell you?
5. What kinds of activities allow you to exercise within your working range?

VARIATION

The exact formula for computing *working range* is available on numerous Internet sites. For an additional challenge, have the students locate the formula and individually compute their exact working range.

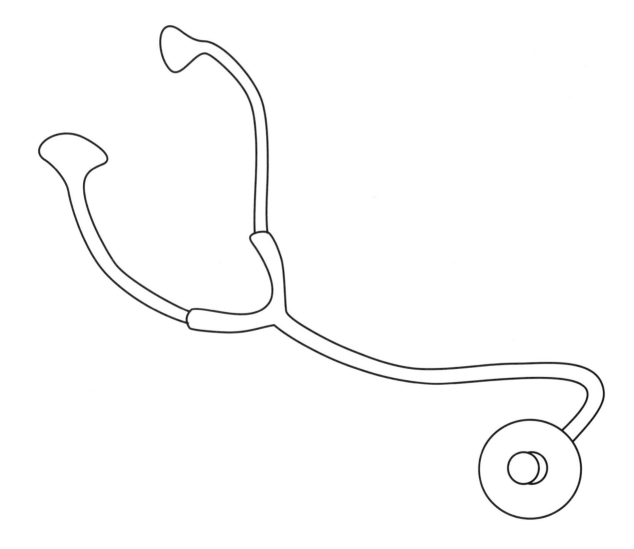

Exercise

HITTING THE TARGET RANGE
EXPERIENCE SHEET

You will be timed while you exercise. After each two-minute exercise period, measure your pulse rate. Record the measurements below.

1. Record your *resting* pulse rate: _____

2. Record your *working* range: _____ to _____

3. Stand and run in place for one minute.

4. Immediately take your pulse rate and record it here: _____

5. Record your pulse rate during 10 minutes of exercise at intervals of two minutes. Your leader will time you.

   Heart rate after two minutes: _____

   Heart rate after four minutes: _____

   Heart rate after six minutes: _____

   Heart rate after eight minutes: _____

   Heart rate after 10 minutes: _____

6. Record your *recovery* pulse rate: _____

   I exercised within my working heart-rate range ____ yes ____ no

   An activity that I enjoy that allows me to exercise within my range is: _____

   _____

 Less Student Stress, More School Success

REACH FOR THE BEST
STRETCHING VISUALIZATION

OBJECTIVES   Students will:
- Reduce stress with easy stretching and visualization.

MATERIALS   Optional CD of light music conducive to slow, rhythmic stretching

DIRECTIONS   Tell the students that you will read a script that involves both stretching and visualizing, and that you would like them to follow along and do what you are suggesting. Ask the students to stand in a comfortable position where they will not bump into desks, chairs, or one another. Start the music (optional) and slowly read from the script, pausing briefly between instructions.

Stand comfortably, with your feet approximately shoulder-width apart. Imagine that you are in a beautiful fruit orchard ... There are many, many fruit trees here. In front of you is a tree with your very favorite fruit ... Slowly reach up with one arm and stretch as far as you can to reach a piece of the fruit ... Lift your opposite heel off the ground as you are stretching ... Pretend you are reaching for a plump, ripe, juicy orange, apple, peach, or other fruit ... Now, reach with your other arm to pick another piece of fruit that is just a bit farther away, so you must really stretch ... As you are stretching, lift your opposing heel off the ground. This gives you just enough lift to reach that luscious piece of your favorite fruit ... Gently and slowly take those pieces of fruit and lay them on the ground in front of you, flexing your knees slightly as you bend ... Reach and pick again. This time stretch even further to get the best looking piece of fruit ... Shift your reaching from arm to arm, always lifting the opposite heel while keeping your toe on the ground ... After every few reaches, lay the fruit on the ground ... Now, pick up a piece of your favorite fruit and take a big bite ... Enjoy the taste. It is sweet and juicy and good for your body ... As you eat the fruit, say to yourself, "I feel so good" ... "This fruit is good for me" ... "I love to eat foods that are healthy" ... After you have picked one more beautiful pieces of fruit, stretching as far as you possibly can, pick up your fruit and take it with you to your seat.

DISCUSSION QUESTIONS
1. How did it feel to stretch your body?
2. Stretching builds flexibility. Why is flexibility important?
3. What kind of fruit were you "picking?" How did it "taste?"
4. Did visualizing the orchard make the stretching more fun? How?

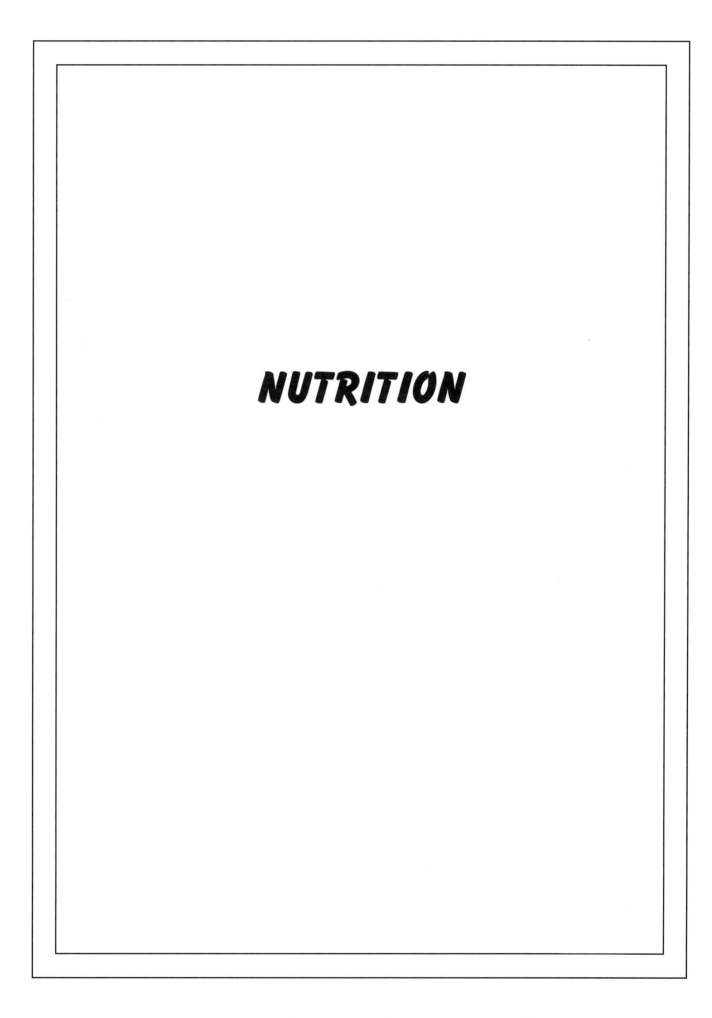

NUTRITION

PYRAMID MENU PLANNING
EXPERIENCE SHEETS AND DISCUSSION

OBJECTIVES Students will:
- Explain the organization and meaning of the Healthy Eating Pyramid.
- Assign foods eaten to locations on the pyramid and evaluate the results.
- Use the pyramid to plan meals and snacks for one day.

MATERIALS One copy of the "Healthy Eating Pyramid" experience sheet for each student; one copy of the "Menu Planning" experience sheet for each student; overhead projector (optional)

DIRECTIONS Begin by asking the students what they have eaten so far today. List both foods and beverages on the board. Get as much input as you can, recording duplications as check marks after various items.

Distribute the "Healthy Eating Pyramid" experience sheets. Either draw a simplified pyramid on the board, or project the graphic from the experience sheet, using an overhead projector.

Starting at the bottom of the pyramid (the foundation of exercise and weight control) discuss the various categories and the implications of their size and placement. A strength of this pyramid is that it does not dictate the number of portions in any category, but conveys relative amounts graphically. For example, it's easy to see that fruits/vegetables and whole grains are equal in size and are the most important categories.

Go through the list on the board and ask the students to decide in which category each item belongs. Using the graphic on the board or overhead, run tallies next to each category. When you have finished, let the students interpret the results. Ask volunteers to explain what the tallies say about the eating behavior of the class so far that day.

Distribute the "Menu Planning" experience sheets. Working in pairs, have the students develop menus that follow the pyramid guidelines. Circulate and offer assistance, as needed. When the students have finished their menus, ask volunteers to describe meals from their plans and explain how they comply with the pyramid. Facilitate discussion.

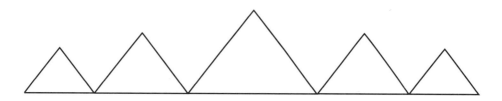

DISCUSSION QUESTIONS

1. Why is exercise part of the pyramid's foundation?
2. What are your favorite vegetables? What's a veggie you've never tried?
3. What are good fats?
4. What are the next largest categories after vegetables/fruits and whole grains?
5. Which does the guide tell you to eat more of, fish or hot dogs? Why?
6. What was the hardest thing about planning menus that follow the pyramid?
7. In order to follow the pyramid, how do you need to change your eating habits?

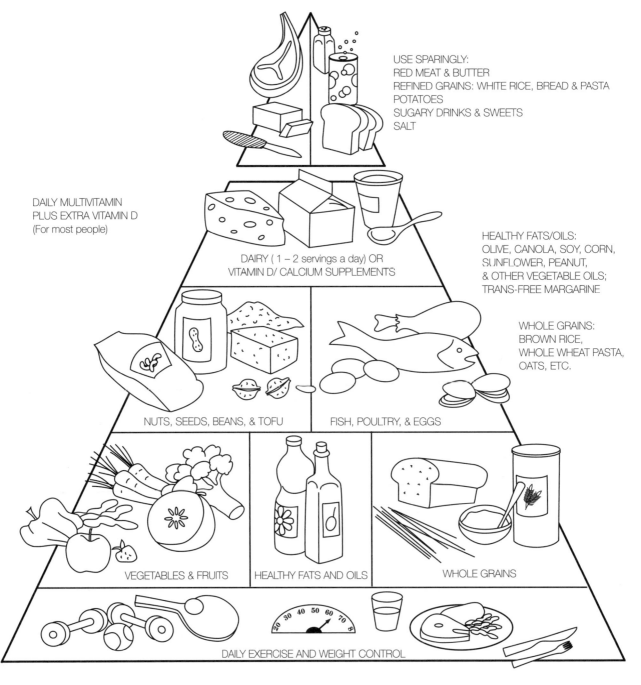

USE SPARINGLY:
RED MEAT & BUTTER
REFINED GRAINS: WHITE RICE, BREAD & PASTA
POTATOES
SUGARY DRINKS & SWEETS
SALT

DAILY MULTIVITAMIN
PLUS EXTRA VITAMIN D
(For most people)

DAIRY (1 – 2 servings a day) OR
VITAMIN D/ CALCIUM SUPPLEMENTS

HEALTHY FATS/OILS:
OLIVE, CANOLA, SOY, CORN,
SUNFLOWER, PEANUT,
& OTHER VEGETABLE OILS;
TRANS-FREE MARGARINE

WHOLE GRAINS:
BROWN RICE,
WHOLE WHEAT PASTA,
OATS, ETC.

NUTS, SEEDS, BEANS, & TOFU

FISH, POULTRY, & EGGS

VEGETABLES & FRUITS

HEALTHY FATS AND OILS

WHOLE GRAINS

DAILY EXERCISE AND WEIGHT CONTROL

HEALTHY EATING PYRAMID
EXPERIENCE SHEET

USE SPARINGLY:
RED MEAT & BUTTER
REFINED GRAINS: WHITE RICE, BREAD & PASTA
POTATOES
SUGARY DRINKS & SWEETS
SALT

DAILY MULTIVITAMIN
PLUS EXTRA VITAMIN D
(For most people)

DAIRY (1 – 2 servings a day) OR
VITAMIN D/ CALCIUM SUPPLEMENTS

HEALTHY FATS/OILS:
OLIVE, CANOLA, SOY, CORN,
SUNFLOWER, PEANUT,
& OTHER VEGETABLE OILS;
TRANS-FREE MARGARINE

WHOLE GRAINS:
BROWN RICE,
WHOLE WHEAT PASTA,
OATS, ETC.

NUTS, SEEDS, BEANS, & TOFU

FISH, POULTRY, & EGGS

VEGETABLES & FRUITS

HEALTHY FATS AND OILS

WHOLE GRAINS

DAILY EXERCISE AND WEIGHT CONTROL

Remember:

1. Get lots of exercise.

2. Learn to love fruits and vegetables.

3. Eat whole-grain cereals and breads.

4. Nuts and seeds are great in small amounts.

5. Choose fish over meat.

6. Eat low or no-fat dairy products.

7. Cut down on sugar, salt, red meat and most baked goods.

MENU PLANNING
EXPERIENCE SHEET

Plan all of your meals and snacks for one day. Include appropriate amounts from different levels of the Healthy Eating Pyramid. Do the best you can to make your menu match the pyramid.

BREAKFAST

_____
_____
_____
_____

SNACK

_____
_____
_____
_____

LUNCH

_____
_____
_____
_____

SNACK

_____
_____
_____
_____

DINNER

_____
_____
_____
_____

SNACK

_____
_____
_____
_____

Less Student Stress, More School Success

THE BREAKFAST BOOST

EXPERIENCE SHEET AND DISCUSSION

OBJECTIVES   Students will:
- Describe the benefits of eating breakfast.
- Develop breakfast ideas that fit the Healthy Eating Pyramid.

MATERIALS   One copy of the experience sheet "The Breakfast Pyramid" for each student

DIRECTIONS   Ask for a show of hands from students who ate breakfast today. Invite several of the responders to describe what they had to eat. Encourage the class to comment by asking questions, such as, "Was that a healthy breakfast?" "What was the healthiest thing about that breakfast?" and "How could you change that breakfast to make it more nutritious?"

Discuss the benefits of eating a healthy breakfast. Involve the students as much as possible. For example, if you have students who eat breakfast some mornings, but not others, ask them to describe any differences between the way they feel with and without breakfast. Point out that, in general, students who eat breakfast:
- Perform better in school.
- Get higher grades on tests.
- Have more energy for sports and other activities.
- Eat less for lunch (good for weight control).
- Don't have as many behavior problems as kids who don't eat breakfast.

Ask the students to name foods that can be part of a nutritious breakfast. Among traditional breakfast foods, include fruit, cereals, egg dishes, toast, juice, and milk. Encourage students to name nontraditional foods that could be eaten for breakfast as well. Don't be afraid to get creative.

Distribute the experience sheets. Working in pairs, have the students illustrate their blank Healthy Eating Pyramids with drawings of foods that make up healthy breakfasts. Have them display their finished pyramids and briefly discuss each one. If you like, have the class vote for the "tastiest," "healthiest," and "most unusual."

DISCUSSION QUESTIONS
1. What healthy foods did you include in your breakfast?
2. In how many parts of the pyramid did you have foods?
3. How can breakfast help you do better in school?
4. What is something nutritious that you can eat when you are in a hurry?
5. What kinds of bread make the most nutritious toast?

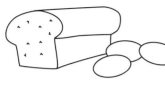

THE BREAKFAST PYRAMID
EXPERIENCE SHEET

DIRECTIONS:

1. Working with your partner, come up with ideas for a healthy breakfast.
2. Decide where each food goes on the pyramid. Include every part of the meal.
3. Draw a picture of the food in the appropriate section.

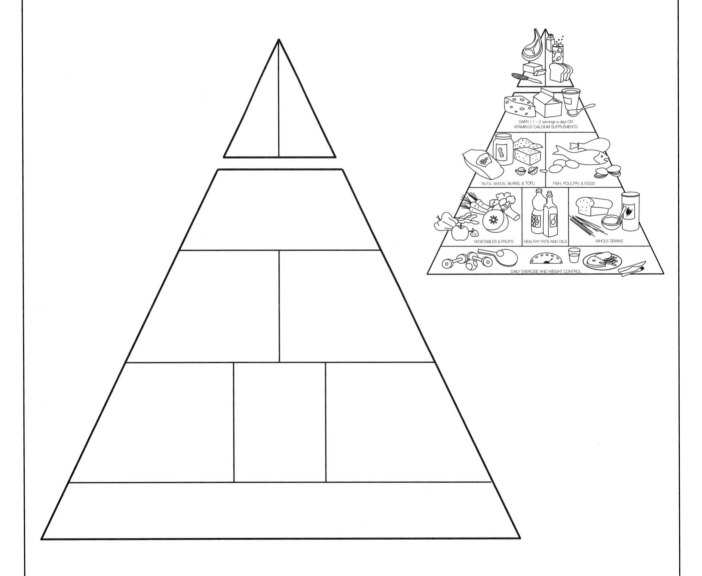

 Less Student Stress, More School Success

LOOKING AT THE FACTS

EXAMINING FOOD LABELS

OBJECTIVES

Students will:
- Examine and compare nutritional and ingredient information on food labels.
- Understand the value of consulting food labels before selecting products.

MATERIALS

Empty food wrappers/containers from a variety of foods, with "Nutritional Facts" panels and ingredient listings intact (one for every two or three students)

DIRECTIONS

Prior to leading this activity, consult the U.S. FDA website (www.FDA.gov and www.FDA.gov/Food/LabelingNutrition) and familiarize yourself with pages devoted to the FDA's Nutritional Facts labeling. The site offers several annotated diagrams that explain how to use the information on the Nutritional Facts panel, including some that can be downloaded and printed for classroom use.

Distribute the empty food wrappers and containers. Depending on the number of samples, have two or three students work together. Read through the labels together. Discuss the meaning of "Serving Size" and "Servings Per Container," and call on several students to read these quantities from their samples. Point out that all the additional items on the label refer to amounts for just one serving.

Continue reading through the labels, comparing amounts of calories, fats, cholesterol, sodium, fiber, sugars, protein, carbohydrates, vitamins, and minerals found in different foods. Discuss the differences between saturated fat and trans fat. Pay particular attention to the number of calories from fat in various foods, as well as the percentages of cholesterol and sodium.

In the process of reading the labels, ask the students to compare the nutritional value of the various foods represented. Have them refer frequently to the list of ingredients to determine where protein, carbohydrates, sodium, trans fat, saturated fat, and other nutritional elements are coming from. Encourage them to get into the habit of reading the labels on foods they buy and eat.

DISCUSSION QUESTIONS

1. If your food wrapper lists trans fat, what ingredients does it probably come from?
2. When you subtract the saturated fats and trans fats from the total fats in a serving, what is left?
3. Why is it a good idea to limit the sodium (salt) in the foods you eat?
4. Based on the information on your food wrapper, does the food it contained belong in a healthy diet? Why or why not?
5. Which of our wrappers held the healthiest food? How do you know?

SNACKING WISELY

EXPERIENCE SHEET AND DISCUSSION

OBJECTIVES   Students will:
- Explain the benefits of healthy snacking.
- Brainstorm nutritious snack foods.
- Develop snack menus for one week.

MATERIALS   One copy of the experience sheet "Snack Attack" for each student

DIRECTIONS   Explain to the students that since snacking often occurs spontaneously, it is important to think ahead and prepare to satisfy sudden hunger pangs with healthy snacks. Otherwise, old habits take over, like reaching for a bag of salty chips, or grabbing a candy bar from the nearest vending machine.

If the students completed the menu-planning activity, remind them that snacks were planned right along with regular meals. Explain:

Snacking between meals is not a bad thing. In fact, it is often essential for maintaining energy levels when meals are more than four or five hours apart. Snacking gets a bad rap because snack foods are often high in calories and salt and low in nutrients. When you fill up on unhealthy snacks and then skip balanced meals, you do yourself no favors. But when you eat nutritious, relatively low-calorie snacks, you benefit from the energy boost without spoiling your appetite for the next regular meal. And you don't have to worry about gaining excess weight.

Ask the students to help you brainstorm a list of nutritious snacks. Write suggestions on the board. List all suggestions. Examples: plain popcorn, whole-grain crackers with peanut butter, unsweetened fruit juices, fresh fruits and vegetables, low-fat yogurt and cheese, raisins and other dried fruit, unsalted nuts and seeds.

After brainstorming, go back over the final list and talk about questionable items, particularly snacks that might contain large amounts of sugar, salt, or fat. For example, a typical bakery muffin is made with white flour (not whole grain), is high in sugar, and may contain trans fats, which are even worse for the heart and blood vessels than saturated fats, such as butter and lard. After discussing an unhealthy snack, cross it off the list.

If computers are available, ask teams of students to research the "bad" ingredients that you have been urging them to avoid. Have them read and report on the effects of sugar, salt, saturated fats, and trans fats on the body.

Distribute the experience sheets and discuss the assignment. Encourage the students to be specific when making their choices. For example, instead of listing "fruit" as a snack, they should describe the type and amount of fruit, such as "1 apple," or "large bunch of grapes."

Ask volunteers to read their snack lists to the class. Facilitate discussion.

DISCUSSION QUESTIONS
1. What kinds of snacks are available from most vending machines?
2. Where can you find healthy snacks?
3. What kinds of snack foods does your family keep at home?
4. What can you do to improve your own snacking habits?

 # SNACK ATTACK
EXPERIENCE SHEET

PLAN NUTRITIOUS SNACKS FOR FIVE DAYS.

. . . .

Monday

Midmorning _____

Afternoon _____

Evening _____

. . . .

Tuesday

Midmorning _____

Afternoon _____

Evening _____

. . . .

Wednesday

Midmorning _____

Afternoon _____

Evening _____

. . . .

Thursday

Midmorning _____

Afternoon _____

Evening _____

. . . .

Friday

Midmorning _____

Afternoon _____

Evening _____

. . . .

 Less Student Stress, More School Success

CHANGING EATING HABITS
EXPERIENCE SHEET AND DISCUSSION

OBJECTIVES   Students will:
- Describe specific ways they could improve their eating habits.
- Explain how habits are formed and broken.
- Identify foods that need to be increased or eliminated from their diets.

MATERIALS   One copy of the experience sheet "Room for Change" for each student

DIRECTIONS   Ask for a show of hands from students who believe their eating habits could use some improvement. Encourage them to consider all the information they've learned about food groups, menu planning, and nutritional ingredients, as well as what they know from other sources about a healthy lifestyle and the dangers of obesity, and the kinds of eating habits that contribute to both.

Ask volunteers to describe one or two improvements they could make. Ask questions to help them zero in on possible behavior changes within their control. For example, if a student says, "I need to cut down on soft drinks," ask "How many a day do you drink?" "Where do you get them?" "Do you drink them because you are thirsty, because you crave something sweet, or out of habit?" and "What could you drink, eat, or do instead?"

In the process of the discussion, point out that a lot of eating occurs from habit (they aren't called "eating habits" for nothing). We tend to make the same food choices over and over again, without giving them much thought. This is particularly true of snacks. Over time, we get to thinking we can't survive without a daily fix of french fries, or chocolate, or soda.

Explain that the way to change a habit is to deliberately and consciously substitute something else for the thing you want to reduce or eliminate. So, instead of drinking a soft drink, you could deliberately choose water or a piece of fruit. Or you could change your routine, so that the event that triggers the desire for a soft drink doesn't occur.

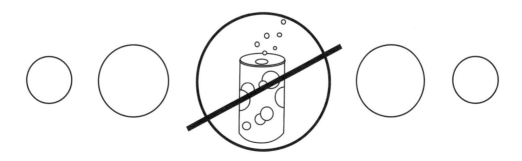

Distribute the experience sheets and go over the directions. Emphasize that students who really want to change their eating habits must think carefully about "how" they plan to break old habits and incorporate new behaviors. For example, if they write that they need to eat more vegetables, where will those vegetables come from and what meals will include them?

Ask volunteers to read some of what they wrote to the class. Facilitate discussion.

DISCUSSION QUESTIONS

1. Who can help you to change your eating habits?
2. How will you benefit by making the changes you described?
3. How does something become a habit?
4. Why are habits so difficult to break?
5. How can eating healthier foods help you in school?

Less Student Stress, More School Success

ROOM FOR CHANGE
EXPERIENCE SHEET

Think carefully about your eating habits, particularly snacks and other foods you tend to eat often. Decide which foods you need to …

1. Add to your diet, or eat more of.
2. Remove from your diet, or eat less of.
3. Continue eating in about the same amounts.

Finally, write down *how* you plan to make the change. Deciding you should do (or stop doing) something usually isn't enough to make it happen. You need a plan.

ADD	HOW?
_____	_____
_____	_____
_____	_____
_____	_____

REMOVE	HOW?
_____	_____
_____	_____
_____	_____

CONTINUE

_____

_____

_____

ABOUT THE AUTHORS

Instructional designers Susanna Palomares and Dianne Schilling have enjoyed a more than twenty-year collaboration writing and producing K–12 educational materials for teachers and counselors. Together they have published dozens of creative, practical activity guides addressing topics in the social-emotional development and life-skills domains.

Susanna Palomares

Dianne Schilling